International perspectives on adult and continuing education

Edited by Peter Jarvis, University of Surrey
Consultant Editors: Chris Duke and Ettore Gelpi

Training adult educators in Western Europe

What does 1992 mean for educators of adults?
How do the different national systems compare?

This book is a comparative study of systems of preparing adult educators in the major European countries. It provides essential reference material on funding, provision and cultural orientation in the Benelux countries, France and the Mediterranean, the German-speaking countries, Scandinavia, the United Kingdom and Eire.

Traditionally, there has been little formal preparation and no certification required for teaching adults. Subject knowledge, enthusiasm and common sense have been considered the important qualifications. The contributors to this book argue that, although this approach has helped avoid the development of a closed profession, training has often been minimal and teaching of variable quality. As the European socio-economic community takes shape and the opportunities and requirements for adult learning increase — particularly in business and language ability — it is becoming clear that there needs to be more Europe-wide specialist training and evaluation in teaching and management skills.

The book provides an excellent resource for adult education professionals and includes guidance on provision, training requirements and further information.

Peter Jarvis is Reader, and **Alan Chadwick** is a Deputy Head of the Department of Educational Studies, both at the University of Surrey.

Training adult educators in Western Europe

Edited by
Peter Jarvis and Alan Chadwick

Published by Routledge in association with the
European Bureau of Adult Education

First published in 1991
by Routledge
11 New Fetter Lane, London EC4P 4EE

Simultaneously published in the USA and Canada
by Routledge
a division of Routledge, Chapman and Hall Inc.
29 West 35th Street, New York, NY 10001

Wordprocessed by Amy Boyle Word Processing
Printed and bound in Great Britain by
Biddles Ltd, Guildford and King's Lynn

British Library Cataloguing in Publication Data
Training adult educators in Western Europe. - (International
    perspectives on adult and continuing education).
    1. Great Britain. Adult education institutions. Teachers.
    Professional education
    I. Jarvis, Peter 1937- II. Chadwick, A.F. (Alan F.)
    III. Series
    370.7120941
    ISBN 0–415–01882–X

Library of Congress Cataloging in Publication Data
Training adult educators in western Europe/edited by Peter Jarvis
    and Alan Chadwick.
    p. cm. - (International perspectives on adult and
    continuing education)
    Includes bibliographical references and index.
    ISBN 0–415–01882–X
    1. Adult education teachers - Training of - Europe - Cross-
    cultural studies. 2. Adult education - Europe - Cross-cultural
    studies.
    I. Jarvis, Peter. II. Chadwick, A.F. (Alan F.) III. European
    Bureau of Adult Education. IV. Series.
    LC5225.T4T68 1992
    374'.94–dc20   90-45428
                                                              CIP

This book is dedicated to
all those who devote time to the
education and training of adults
throughout the whole of Europe

Contents

Contents

Contents

Tables

The contributors

José A. Valcárcel Amador is an adult educator and a member of the Colectivo Taller de Cultura y Educación Popular — the School for Life — Madrid. He has also worked in popular education in America.

Bill Bax is the Secretary General of the European Bureau of Adult Education.

Sanneke Bolhuis is a member of the Advisory Council for Adult Education in the Netherlands.

Hallgjerd Brattset is currently senior lecturer in the Norwegian Armed Forces Psychological and Education Centre, and holds a masters degree in psychology and education. Over the years she has served on many committees, including the Norwegian Institute of Adult Education, and has represented Norway in international conferences on adult education. She has also lectured at different universities in Norway on a part-time basis and taught for a short period at the University of Liverpool, UK.

José M. Quintana Cabanas is Professor of social pedagogy at the Autónoma University, Barcelona, Spain. He is the author of several books on social pedagogy.

Alan Chadwick is currently Deputy Head of the Department of Educational Studies at the University of Surrey, and holds two higher degrees in adult education. He has served on a number of national committees concerned with the education of adults, including those associated with the National Institute of Adult Continuing Education. For over twenty years he has conducted research and published in adult education and has worked as a teacher and trainer in numerous settings in the United Kingdom and abroad. He is, at present, Director of the Surrey University Centre for Commonwealth and European Education and Development.

Paolo Federighi is professor of adult education in the University of Florence and a well-known writer on adult education in Italy.

Pierre Freynet studied philosophy at the University of Tours obtaining both a Licentiate and a Master's degree in 1968 and 1969 respectively and a doctorate from the University of Caen on university continuing education. Since 1977 he has been director of the University of Angers Centre for Continuing Education. He has published a number of papers on the struggle against illiteracy, and has completed a UNESCO study on literacy education in France. In addition, he was a participant in the Geiranger Conference organised by the European Bureau on the preparation of adult educators, and is actively engaged in the training of trainers in literacy education.

Ivan Häuser is the Head of the Centre for Teachers in Adult Education in Aarhus, Denmark. He has a higher degree in Russian and Czech, is a former education adviser in languages to teachers in voluntary education and a teacher on single-subject courses for examination.

Huib Hinnekint has been working at the Centre for Andragogical Research in Brussels since 1963. He has been involved in the training of adult educators in different settings over a number of years and also in the development of curricula and training policies. From 1975 to 1981 he was engaged in setting up the 'Open School' project in the Netherlands. He has published widely in the field of adult education.

Declan Irvine is Senior Lecturer in Education, University College, Galway, Eire. He was formerly lecturer at the Institute of Extension Studies, University of Liverpool. His subjects include sociology of education, international issues in education and adult education. His research interests encompass the professionalism of teaching and access to university for mature students. His publications include articles on adult literacy, teacher education, the training of adult educators and nurse education. He has just completed a report on nurse education for the Department of Health and hopes to complete a book on adult education in the near future.

Peter Jarvis is Reader in the Education of Adults at the University of Surrey. He has published many books and papers on a variety of adult eduction subjects, including the Houle Award-winning *Adult Learning in the Social Context*. He has recently published the first *International Dictionary of Adult and Continuing Education* and is currently working on a number of other books, including *Paradoxes of Human Learning*, and co-editing, for the American Association for Adult and Continuing Education, a book entitled *Adult Education as a Field of Study: its evolution, achievements and future*. This is to be published in the USA in 1990. Additionally, he is co-editor of *The International Journal of Lifelong Education*, editor of the two series of books on adult education published by Routledge: *International Adult Education* and *Theory and Practice of Adult Education in North America*. His work has now been translated into a number of languages and he is a frequent speaker and lecturer both in the United Kingdom and abroad.

Yngye Kasimir is an administrator and planner for the folk high school teacher training programme at Linköping University, Sweden, and studied social science at the Universities of Lund and Umeå. He was a teacher in a folk high school and has taught methodology at the Teacher Training College at Linköping. He is active in Christian, trades union and political voluntary organisations.

Ursula Knitter-Lux is the general secretary of the Vienna Association of Popular Culture.

Derek Legge is an internationally known adult educator who joined the University of Manchester in 1946, was appointed to the new Department of Adult Education there in 1949 and retired as its head in 1976. He has served on many committees. He was the first individual member of the European Bureau of Adult Education and is a frequent contributor to books and journals. His major publication is *The Education of Adults in Britain* which was brought out by the Open University Press in 1982.

Carl Rohrer is currently assistant secretary of the Swiss Federation of Adult Education.

Klitos Symeonides holds an MA degree in adult education and is president of the Pan-Cyprian Committee on Adult Education.

Dimitris Vergidis was born in 1950 in Kavala, Greece. He has studied education in Paris and worked for the Greek Ministry of National Economy and was general secretary for popular education. In 1987 he was appointed to the planning committee of the new University of Thessalia. He has written a number of chapters in books and articles on popular education.

Joke Wagenaar is a research worker in the field of adult education in Nijmegen in the Netherlands.

Johannes Weinberg is Professor of Adult and Out of School Youth Education at the University of Munster. He has published in the fields of social history of adult education, adult education and the trades unions, adult learning and the training and re-training of adult educators.

Pentti Yrjölä is currently senior inspector in the Department of Adult Education, National Board of General Education, Helsinki, Finland. He was pedagogic direct of Kansanvalistusseura (the Society for Popular Culture) in Finland, and also editor of *Adult Education in Finland, The Yearbook of Liberal Adult Education* and also of *Aikuiskasvatus* (Adult Education). He has a masters degree from Tampere University in the Social Sciences and has trained taught in a folk high school and been Secretary General of the Finnish Folk High School Association.

Series editor's note

The Routledge Series on International Perspectives on Adult and Continuing Education brings to an English-speaking readership a wide overview of developments in the education of adults worldwide. Books are planned for the series of four different types:

a. about adult education in a single country
b. having a comparative perspective of two or more countries
c. having an international perspective
d. symposia of papers for different countries following a single theme.

This book falls into the fourth category and it is an important contribution to the literature because it contains case studies from the greater majority of Western European countries. It is the first single volume in the education of adults which seeks to cover all of Western Europe, an increasingly important approach with the advent of The Single European Market in 1992.

The theme of training adult educators is also appropriate at this time as an increasing number of organisations are recognising the need to prepare professionally those who teach adults. It is, in many ways, a companion volume to that prepared by Stephen Brookfield, entitled *Training Educators of Adults*, which appeared in the parallel series of books on the *Theory and Practice of Adult Education in North America*, also published by Routledge.

Peter Jarvis
Series Editor

Preface

There can be little doubt that opportunities for the education of adults in Western Europe are now becoming an area of growth. As the field has grown and developed, it has even acquired a variety of different names in different countries, so that even the term *adult education* is not agreed universally throughout Western Europe, as readers will discover in the following pages. The editors' understanding of the term is broad, to include popular education and vocational preparation. This latter aspect of adult education, namely training, has taken its place on political agendas. Nevertheless, international organisations as well as governments are, to varying degrees, recognising the significance of offering personal and vocational education and training to adults beyond the period of initial schooling. Provision is not as widespread or as balanced as many adult educators would wish to see it, nor are opportunities for training yet comprehensive. However, some progress has been made. As school teachers are expected to acquire professional preparation as educators, claims for the training of educators of adults, who work across a wider and at least as challenging a range of groups, are being voiced. Since training on a coherent basis is a relatively new and expanding phenomenon it should be recognised that these case studies provide only an impression, both of initiatives taken in the latter part of the decade, and, concomitantly an opportunity for reflection on issues and questions which still require debate.

The word *training* has a lower status than *education* and so it might perhaps be surprising that the term is still used for the professional preparation of educators of adults. This might reflect the early stage in the growth and development of this form of professional education, but the term is used here to cover every aspect of the vocational preparation of adult educators, from the initial preparation about techniques of teaching adults to postgraduate studies in adult education.

There are, as yet, relatively few studies of educators of adults which focus on their preparation, and even fewer that adopt an international and comparative perspective. Such studies are assuming increasing importance in Western Europe as it moves towards a single market in 1992. This volume seeks to contribute towards this, focusing upon the preparation, development and support of those whose work it is to assist other adults to learn.

The editors fully acknowledge the part played by the European Bureau of Adult Education over a long period of time with regard to this theme and also the commitment brought to this aspect of adult education by individuals and organisations in countries in Western Europe, often against the background of indifference, if not hostility, with regard to questions of policy and resourcing.

The editors have attempted to retain authors' contributions without modification. Where changes were felt to be necessary they have been made only for the purposes of clarification, and occasionally to ensure, wherever possible, that gender neutrality has been maintained.

This book commences with a general introduction and concludes with a chapter which examines some of the common themes and questions drawn from the case studies presented below; these have both been prepared by the editors. A case study from Cyprus has been included (first appendix), which represents its membership of the European Bureau. A second appendix, written by Bill Bax, describes the Bureau's aims and activities.

As Western Europe continues to experience demographic, social and technological changes a requirement for training and the preparation of trainers should increase, not least as existing skills become redundant and the necessity for new ones emerges. It is the editors' hope and intention that this volume should support the contention that educators of adults have much to contribute to this burgeoning area.

Peter Jarvis
Alan Chadwick

Acknowledgements

The editors wish to thank the European Bureau of Adult Education for its co-operation and support, and for being almost wholly successful in eliciting a full and representative set of contributions from the countries of Western Europe.

Particular thanks must go to Bill Bax, General Secretary of the Bureau, for his continuing encouragement, and to Peter Clyne, formerly Chair of the Executive Committee of the Bureau, for his active support and for liaising between the editors and the Executive Committee. Thanks are due to Elenore Arthur, Pam Denicolo and Charles Hancock, for translating part of the Swiss chapter and the chapters from Italy and Austria respectively.

In conclusion, the editors are very grateful to all the authors for their contributions to the growing debate surrounding training for educators of adults.

1   Towards a theoretical rationale

Peter Jarvis

> Most leadership training, like most adult education, is self-directed. An individual confronted with the responsibility of becoming an educator of adults learns partly by the process of participation and partly by his [*sic*] own examination of that process. He studies books or pamphlets or manuals, he talks with others in a similar situation, he goes to meetings, he asks for supervisory assistance, he visits other programs, or he analyzes his own performance in terms of a standard which he has developed himself or adopted from some other source. The quality of his learning depends in essence upon his capacity to teach himself.
>
> (Houle 1960: 118)

It is perhaps significant that in the year before Houle's (1961) seminal study on self-directed learning was published, he was already claiming that those who were entering adult education in America were expected to be self-directed since little provision for professional preparation was made for them, whether they were volunteers, part-time leaders or adult education specialists. Indeed, Liveright (1964: 93) recognised that adult education was not a profession that most adult educators had not 'participated in an organized program of graduate study . . . [and were] action rather than research oriented.' But by 1985 the picture had most certainly changed:

> Today, there is a profound need to train new and existing personnel in a manner congruent with the field. . . . the plea for properly trained personnel has become a full-fledge chorus in most parts of the world.
>
> (Boshier 1985: 3)

Indeed, this is a picture that most adult educators will recognise as being fairly true to the late 1980s and indeed the American Commission of Professors of Adult Education has already

1

discussed the standards that should be found in graduate programmes in adult education (see Brookfield 1988: 234-41), and yet this movement has not been without its opponents. It is not uncommon to hear adult educators expressing the desire to have training and yet not wanting to prevent volunteers and others wishing to teach their hobbies (the 'apprentices' — Graham *et al*. 1982) from embarking upon teaching adults, especially if they appear to have a natural aptitude for it. Indeed, the openness of adult education for enthusiasts to enter the field has always been an element of its ethos. Hence it is not surprising that some adult educators have counselled caution in this apparent movement towards professionalisation. (See Carlson 1972, 1977; Ohliger 1974). Others, such as Illich *et al*. (1977), have also viewed professionalisation as a phenomenon that is not to be encouraged.

However, the movement has occurred and the professional preparation of educators of adults is beginning to appear in many countries of the world and, naturally, this has led to a number of studies of the process, such as that by Graham *et al*. (1982) in the United Kingdom. However, there have been a very few comparative studies, such as that published by the European Bureau of Adult Education (1982) and that published by the International Council for Adult Education (Boshier 1985).

Hence, this study fits into this trend; its opening chapter has three main purposes. Initially, in a study such as this one it is necessary to set the adult education scene so that it is possible to understand this process of professionalisation against a broader backcloth. This is undertaken here through a sociological analysis of the development of a profession. One model of professionalisation is employed, although it is recognised that any single model over-simplifies the process, but as the aim of the chapter is not an exploration in the sociology of professions, but an analysis of the process of social change in adult education this is not regarded as a hindrance to comprehension (but see Jarvis 1985: 227-41). The second purpose is to relate this study to the increasing awareness of the field of international comparative adult education. Reference is made here both to some of the contemporary movements within it and some of the studies which have emerged in recent years. While this study is regarded as part of that trend, there is also another factor that makes it important; by 1992 Western Europe will have moved into an even closer political-economic community and there is a growing necessity for Europeans everywhere to understand their own cultural heritages so that there can be a process of mutual learning. In the third section there is a short review of some of

2

the contemporary studies of the preparation of adult educators. Finally, there is a brief concluding discussion.

TOWARDS THE PROFESSIONALISATION OF EDUCATORS OF ADULTS

Houle (1960) made the point that the majority of adult educators in America were either volunteers or part-time with only a few being full-time and yet Wilensky (1970: 487) claimed that the first stage in professionalisation is 'to start doing full time the thing that needs doing'. If this is the first stage of professionalisation, then it might be claimed that adult education has not begun to professionalise. However, other alternatives present themselves, such as the possibility that Wilensky's model is not correct in the case of adult education, or even that adult education is unique among occupations because it might never have a majority of full-time members. Indeed, it will be shown that Wilensky's model is too simple for such fields of practice as adult education and that it is necessary to expand his analysis in order to make it relevant to adult education.

Wilensky assumed that there is a direct correlation between an occupation and a profession but it is suggested here that such an assumption cannot be made in the case of adult education, because it is not a single occupation. This is also one of the weaknesses in Houle's (1960) well-known paper on adult educators when he claimed that there were few specialist adult educators because he omitted from his considerations those people who spend the greater part of their professional lives educating adults but in professions other than education, such as nursing, medicine, etc., although he (1980) was later to write a major book on the professions and their continuing education. Educators of adults may be members of other occupations and professions, and act as educators within the framework of those other professions, or they may be volunteers or part-time tutors who teach on a part-time basis and who may, but need not, be members of other occupations or professions. The irony of the situation is such that those who are full-time adult educators, specialists according to Houle, may actually be administrators of the educational service rather than teachers within it. Hence the majority of those who teach may be part-time in this occupation, some may be members of other occupations and professions, while those who are full-time adult educators may not be teachers. Therefore, the simple correlation drawn by Wilensky between an occupation and a profession may over-simplify the reality of the situation and the growth in preparation of adult educators may represent a process in professionalisation which Wilensky did not consider — that of the professionalisation of a full-time and part-time field of practice simultaneously.

This raises another problem: that of.deciding precisely what is meant by adult education and similar terms and how these relate to fields of practice in different countries. Thus far the terms *adult education* and *educators of adults* have been used synonymously although they do convey different conceptions of the process: the former, for instance is often used in respect of adult liberal education whilst the latter has a much wider connotation. The use of the former term was one of the problems in this study which is referred to in the Preface, where the representatives of one country claimed not to have adult education in their country although popular education and professional education, etc., certainly exist there — i.e. education for adults! There can be no simple definition here because the authors of the different chapters employ concepts according to the practice of their own society so that the context must determine the precise meaning.

Wilensky's discussion of the second stage in the process is extremely relevant to this study in particular and to adult education in general, since it refers to the desire of an occupation to start training and to establish a training school and then to seek to re-locate it in a university, if the school was not originally based in one. It will be seen in the following chapters that this is the situation which is occurring in adult education in Western Europe, with some professional preparation being in higher education, but much outside of it.

The significance of this stage in professionalisation is in constructing a systematic body of knowledge about the field of practice. While research often provides new understanding and quite specific knowledge about aspects of the field of practice, it does not provide a rationale for building up a body of knowledge about it. That occurs in professional preparation when all the knowledge that has been gathered through research and experience, both within and about the field of practice, is systematised into a curriculum which is taught to those about to enter the field, or who are already in it. Clearly this is a significant stage for this study since it is possible to see the body of knowledge about adult education growing and developing as the curricula for professional preparation are examined. Hence the reasons why American adult education has placed so much emphasis upon the standard of graduate programmes in adult education can be understood (see Jensen *et al.* 1964,

Brookfield 1988 *inter alia*).

Additionally, there has always been some discussion in adult education as to whether preparation for adult teaching should occur before employment or as an in-service exercise. Caldwell (1981: 8) points out that in America: 'A review of the literature reveals that beyond formal university degree programs in adult and continuing education, pre-service training programs are not common.' Indeed, the study of adult education in America has tended to concentrate on graduate in-service programmes rather than undergraduate pre-service preparation, but this study will show how the process has differed in various countries in Western Europe.

Wilensky went on to highlight subsequent stages in the process of professionalisation, leading to the formation of a professional organisation. But it might be claimed that each society in Western Europe has its own adult education association, and that each has contributed to this book, so that it cannot be a final stage in the process. This is true, but the extent to which the adult education associations whose members have contributed to this book are actually professional associations, in the way that Wilensky implied, is a much more debatable point. The fact, however, remains that their existence demonstrates that Wilensky's discussion of professionalisation is not totally relevant and that the process of change in the education of adults that is being studied here is much more complex than this model, or other models of professionalisation, tend to imply.

Consequently, it is pertinent to ask whether the process of change that is recorded here is actually one of professionalisation or merely one of change. That there is some change in the same direction in adult education in most countries tends to suggest that there is a deliberate movement towards certain ideals for adult education as an occupation in different countries, and these include occupational preparation and the consequent emergence of a body of knowledge. It is concluded, therefore, that this process of change is in accord with what is generally regarded as professionalisation, even though the occupation, or occupations, is much more complex than generally assumed. Even more significantly, it is suggested that because of the nature of adult education professionalisation is occurring among part-time practitioners as well as among full-time teachers of adults.

THE EMERGENCE OF COMPARATIVE ADULT EDUCATION

Sociological method is generally regarded as having a comparative basis and the validity of this claim may be seen from the fact that a sociological model was employed here to allow for discussion on the way that the education of adults is developing in an international context.

However, this study is a comparative one and so it is also necessary to place this discussion within that context. From its very earliest organisations adult education has had an international orientation. As early as 1929 there was a World Conference on Adult Education held at Cambridge, United Kingdom and even before that Albert Mansbridge had founded a World Association for Adult Education. These early conferences brought together people who were interested in adult education and it enabled them to see what each other was doing. It was not really until 1966, however, in Exeter, New Hampshire, USA that the comparative aspects of adult education were examined in any detail and here some twenty-five scholars met under the chairmanship of Arthur Adams, of University of New Hampshire, to discuss the comparative study of adult education (Liveright and Haygood 1968).

Since then there has been both the growth in international organisations, such as the European Bureau of Adult Education and the International Council for Adult Education, but these provide a forum for practitioners and administrators rather than a baseline for academic study of an international and comparative type. Recently, however, a number of international conferences have been organised that have endeavoured to provide the opportunity for comparative international adult education, similar to that provided in Exeter, New Hampshire, and a number of networks of scholars have come into being which are fostering the development of comparative international adult education. However, it is essential at this juncture to make the point that comparative studies need not be international, since comparatives are concerned with the rigorous analysis and comparison of educational policies and processes within countries as well as between them.

In addition a number of significant studies have appeared, such as Harris (1980), Charters *et al.* (1981), Titmus (1981), Charters and Hilton (1989) and Lichtner (1989) and there is considerable research in progress, including that of Knox (see Knox 1987 for an introduction to his work). In the first of the publications referred to here there was an attempt to map the field, whereas the following two were less ambitious in their approach, with Titmus restricting his study to Western Europe. Charters and Hilton, however, have endeavoured to undertake a comparative analysis by setting the format in which the case studies were provided and then analysing them comparatively. By way of contrast, Lichtner has published the papers of an important study seminar on comparative adult education held in 1988 in Frascati. One of the things that most of the authors have done is to use a case study approach from which they endeavoured to draw out significant similarities and differences. However, it must be recognised that this approach has limitations in as much as the authors of the case studies select and classify their data before they are analysed and compared.

The same approach is adopted here and although the framework for the selection was suggested by the editors, it has to be recognised that the chapter authors still made their own data selection which was increased because of the approach adopted by the European Bureau. In this instance the field of study is that of the professional preparation of adult educators in Western Europe. None of the above studies has sought to limit its concern to only one aspect of adult education even though the Charters and Hilton approach limits the case studies to important programmes in adult education. Even a restricted field of study does not, however, overcome the problem of subjective selectivity.

This study does have one predecessor, however, which was undertaken by the European Bureau in 1982, when the newsletter published very short and unsystematic accounts of the professional preparation of adult educators in Western Europe as a preparation for its Geiranger conference. That the topic has already been the subject of a European conference demonstrates the concern that exists among adult educators in Western Europe to understand each other's systems. However, rigorous comparative analysis does more than merely provide an understanding of the different systems, Charters suggests that:

Comparative international adult education has the same basic purposes as adult education and comparative education, fields with which it overlaps. They are, immediately or eventually, to improve the lots and lives of individuals by improving the performance of the educators who help them. Improvement of the educator's performance can come about in two ways. One is by giving them knowledge and skills they can apply directly. The other is by increasing understanding of and information about adult education for its own sake. The debate about the relative values of these two ways is not fruitful because knowledge for its own sake is often translatable into empirically useful knowledge and empirically useful knowledge can increase knowledge for its own sake.

(Charters 1980: 3)

The combination of the theoretical and the practical in Charters's account summarises the main reasons for comparative adult education in general, but with the wider political movement drawing Western Europe closer together there is a degree of urgency for Europeans to understand each others' systems so that co-operation becomes more possible between them. This study provides one small step in that direction in respect of adult education, although it will be clear from the variations in professional preparation that exists in Western Europe that there is a considerable way to go before such systems can be fully integrated, even if such a development was to appear desirable.

SOME PREVIOUS STUDIES OF PROFESSIONAL PREPARATION OF EDUCATORS OF ADULTS

It has already been pointed out that there are few major studies of the preparation of adult educators and many of these are summarised in Jarvis's (1983: 179-210) review of the British literature. However, many of the studies have already been mentioned in this chapter and so a brief overview of it is provided here.

There are at least two ways of looking at this development from an historical perspective: that of the direct preparation of educators of adults or alternatively examining the way that adult education has been studied academically. It is perhaps easier to start with the latter because the former fits into its development. While the first doctorates in adult education in English were awarded in England in the 1920s, it was at Columbia University, New York, USA that the first full doctoral programme began in the mid-1930s. From this programme, and similar later developments on other university campuses in America, a caucus of people with doctoral degrees in adult education began to emerge and to be teachers of adult education within the American university system. By the early 1960s a genuine concern for the future of the subject of adult education in the American universities was emerging, so that by 1960, not only was Houle's (1960) paper published in the *Handbook* (Knowles 1960) but another by Liveright (1960) on adult education in the universities. But the landmark came with the publication of the symposium *Adult Education: Outlines of an Emerging Field of University Study* (Jensen *et al*. 1964) in which many of the leading adult educators in America examined the development of adult education in the university system. In a sense this publication highlighted the fact that there was now sufficient confidence among the American adult educators to assess their own position within higher education. It also illustrates the fact that there were a number of programmes being run in a variety of universities and that many adult education practitioners had studied in them. Since then there has been a concern in America for the quality of these masters and doctoral programmes, as was discussed above, with Brookfield's (1988) book being the culmination of this process until the present, although the American Association is currently undertaking a follow-up study to the Jensen *et al*. publication of 1964.

Unfortunately the American adult education movement has tended, until recently, to be fairly insular in academic terms although extremely open to receiving overseas students to study in its programmes. This has meant that there has not been a great many international or comparative studies on the preparation of adult educators. However, both the international associations mentioned above, the International Council for Adult Education and the European Bureau of Adult Education, have shown some concern for the international comparative aspects. Boshier (1985a) examined the professional preparation of adult educators in a variety of regions in the world and the issue of *Convergence* in which Boshier's article was published contained some excellent case studies, whereas the European Bureau's newsletter made no attempt to provide more than an introduction to the Western European systems. This study is a natural successor to the work which began in the early 1980s.

In the United Kingdom one writer, above all, has concerned himself with this area of work. Elsdon (1975) examined the field of adult education, recording those schemes of training that existed and also making suggestions as to how adult education should develop as a profession. Nearly a decade later he looked at the 'training of trainers', as a great deal of professional preparation in the United Kingdom had emerged outside of the higher education sector (Elsdon 1984). Training of the trainers has not emerged in American adult education because of the prevalence of the university programmes, but it is something that has emerged in adult education in other parts of the world, as will also become clear in some of the following chapters (see also Pick and Yu 1985).

Naturally there have been other research projects on the professional preparation of adult educators (see Graham *et al.* 1982) and the growth and development of research is a logical progression in the professionalisation process.

CONCLUDING DISCUSSION

As occupations professionalise and professional preparation emerges, it becomes a topic for scholastic analysis, adult-education preparation being no exception. However, there have been surprisingly few major works in English about the training of adult educators, and few of them make reference to studies published in other languages, Elsdon (1975) being the notable exception. Indeed, the language barrier is one of the greatest problems for many British and American scholars seeking to study comparative adult education so that much of the academic scholarship in Western Europe and elsewhere tends to be lost to many scholars. However, it is a form of linguistic imperialism to expect scholars, whose first language is not English, to write in it but until such time as technology produces instantaneous translation of the written word, it is necessary to have some means of communication in order to provide a more complete understanding of different cultural systems. It is hoped, therefore, that this study in English of the European system of professional preparation will contribute a little more to this process of understanding.

BIBLIOGRAPHY

Boshier, R. (1985) 'Conceptual framework for analyzing the training of trainers and adult educators', in *Convergence* vol XVIII, nos 3-4.

Boshier, R. (ed.) (1985a) *Training of Trainers and Adult Educators*, Special issue of *Convergence*, XXVIII, nos 3-4.

Brookfield, S. (ed.) (1988) *Training Educators of Adults*, London: Croom Helm.

Caldwell, P.A. (1981) 'Pre-service training for instructors of adults', in S.M. Grabowski *et al.* (1980) *Preparing Educators of Adults*, San Francisco: Jossey Bass Publishers Inc.

Carlson, R. (1972) 'Professional leadership versus the educational service station approach: an historical appraisal', *Adult Education* 23, no. 2.

Carlson, R. (1977) 'Professionalization of adult education: an historical-philosophical analysis', *Adult Education*, 28, no. 1.

Charters, A. *et al.* (1981) *Comparing Adult Education Worldwide*, San Francisco: Jossey Bass Publishers.

Charters, A. and Hilton, R. (eds) (1989) *Landmarks in International Adult Education*, London: Routledge.

Elsdon, K.T. (1975) *Training for Adult Education*, Nottingham: University of Nottingham, Department of Adult Education.

Elsdon, K.T. (1984) *The Training of Trainers*, Nottingham: Huntingdon Publishers Ltd in association with University of Nottingham, Department of Adult Education.

Grabowski, S.M. (1981) *et al. Preparing Educators of Adults*, San Francisco: Jossey Bass Publishers Inc.

Graham, T.B., Daines, J.H., Sullivan, T., Harris, P. and Baum, F.E. (1982) *The Training of Part-Time Teachers of Adults*, Nottingham: University of Nottingham, Dept of Adult Education.

Grusky, O. and Miller, G.A. (eds) (1970) *The Sociology of Organisations: Basic Studies*, New York: The Free Press.

Harris, W.J.A. (1980) *Comparative Adult Education*, London: Longman.

Houle, C.O. (1960) 'The Education of Adult Educational Leaders', in Knowles, M.S. (ed.) (1960) *Handbook of Adult Education in the United States*, Washington: Adult Education Association of the USA.

Houle, C.O. (1961) *The Inquiring Mind*, Madison: University of Wisconsin Press; 2nd edn (1988) Oklahoma City: University of Oklahoma.

Houle, C.O. (1980) *Continuing Learning in the Professions*, San Francisco: Jossey Bass Publishers Inc.

Illich, I., Zola, K.K., McKnight, J., Caplan, J. and Shanken, R. (1977) *Disabling Professions*, London: Marion Boyars.

Jarvis, P. (1983) *Adult and Continuing Education: Theory and Practice*, London: Croom Helm; (1988) republished by Routledge.

Jarvis, P. (1985) *The Sociology of Adult and Continuing Education*, London: Croom Helm.

Jensen, G., Liveright, A.A. and Hallenbeck, W. (eds) (1964) *Adult Education: Outlines of an Emerging Field of University Study*, Washington: Adult Education Association of the United States of America.

Knowles, M.S. (ed.) (1960) *Handbook of Adult Education in the United States*, Washington: Adult Education Association of the USA.

Knox, A. (1987) *International Perspectives on Adult Education*, Columbus, Ohio: ERIC Clearinghouse.

Lichtner, M. (ed.) (1989) *Comparative Research in Adult Education*, Frascati: Centro Europeo Dell' Educazione.

Liveright, A.A. (1960) 'Adult education in colleges and universities', in Knowles, M.S. (ed.) (1960) *Handbook of Adult Education in the United States*, Washington: Adult Education Association of the USA.

Liveright, A.A. (1964) 'The nature and aims of adult education as a field of graduate education', in Jensen, G., Liveright, A.A. and Hallenbeck, W. (eds) (1964) *Adult Education: Outlines of an Emerging Field of University Study*, Washington: Adult Education Association of the United States of America.

Liveright, A.A. and Haygood, N. (eds) (1968) *The Exeter Papers*, Boston: Boston University Center for the Study of Liberal Education for Adults.

Ohliger, J. (1974) 'Is lifelong education a guarantee of permanent inadequacy?' *Convergence* XII, no 2.

Pick, L.H. and Yu, E. (1985) 'Training of trainers in South East Asia', in Boshier R. (ed.) (1985) *Convergence* XVIII, no 3-4.

Titmus, C. (1981) *Strategies for Adult Education: Practices in Western Europe*, Milton Keynes: The Open University Press.

Wilensky, H.L. (1970) 'The professionalization of everyone', reprinted in Grutsky, O. and Miller, G.A. (1970) *The Sociology of Organisations: Basic Studies*.

Wilensky, H.L. (1982) *Newsletter: Training of Adult Educators*, Amersfoort: European Bureau of Adult Education.

Part I

Benelux countries

2   The training of adult educators in Belgium

Huib Hinnekint

ADULT EDUCATION IN BELGIUM

For a better understanding of the training of adult education workers in Belgium it is necessary to start with a historical overview of adult education there.

Belgium was industrialised quite early in the nineteenth century. Partly to meet the great demand for skilled workers an education system evolved which also gave consideration to teaching adults. Evening and Sunday schools were mentioned in the first laws concerning primary and vocational education in 1842. Schooling for adults, which since 1970 has been known as 'schooling for social promotion', is still a very important segment of adult education.

Part of vocational education, especially for adults, takes place outside the school system. This is true for vocational training for shopkeepers and tradespeople, agricultural workers and the unemployed. Special provisions were created for the unemployed after the economic crisis of the 1930s. In addition, many organisations of liberal adult education have emerged over the years. Various social movements, such as the labour movement, the Flemish movement, the Catholic movement and many others have developed in this field. This sector, now known as socio-cultural adult education and which is community education and liberal adult education, is government funded and is still of great importance. Adult education on a private basis completes the list, along with vocational training in offices and factories. These are not regulated by legislation.

Summarising, the following main sectors can be distinguished:

a.   adult education in the school system consists of:
  *   education for social promotion (evening and weekend courses)
  *   correspondence education

- central examinations organised by the state;
b. vocational training for:
  - shopkeepers and tradespeople
  - agricultural workers
  - training and re-training for the unemployed;
c. socio-cultural education (community education or adult liberal education);
d. commercial education and others.

Additionally, there are services for educational broadcasting, educational and vocational guidance, as well as the public libraries. The importance of these services for adult education is still increasing.

THE TRAINING OF ADULT EDUCATORS

Formal adult education

This has the largest number of students, with about 200,000 participants a year. These are mainly language and vocational training courses, not general education. This provision is organised as in general education, at levels corresponding to junior, secondary and higher education, and the same qualifications are required for teaching staff as in youth education. There is no training or refresher training specifically for those working in this sector. Teachers are trained at university or secondary teacher training colleges, where little or no thought is given to training for work in the field of adult education. The fact that there is no specific training may be due to the nature of posts in adult education, which are generally considered to be part-time jobs and this is also the case with managerial and executive positions.

The teaching staff in the vocational training programme for tradespeople are recruited partly from teachers but mostly from merchants and artisans who have an interest in teaching. All must be considered suitable for the work. But for these people, also, their adult education status is as part-time employees. Only the administrator in institutions of this kind is a full-time employee. At national level, however, there is a limited support structure for educational workers. Training and re-training occurs internally by means of seminars, conferences and also through provision of a journal.

Training teachers in agricultural education is seen as less significant, so that adult education is regarded as a part-time activity, like it is in many other sectors of society.

However, it is a different matter in training for the unemployed. Full-time staff are employed here. In December 1980, 1,310 people were employed in this sector of adult education in Belgium, a little over half of them in Flanders. They were recruited following an examination and in 1983, eighty-eight candidates out of the 879 who sat the examination were successful (12.9 per cent). Further training and support of the workers is taken care of by NCPOS (National Centre for Educational Training and Study)[1], an institution especially formed for this purpose within the National Employment Service (RVA). In 1983, it provided 259 training courses for its own staff and a further thirty-one courses for private firms and public institutions.

A third sector of importance for adult education is the socio-cultural sector. This has developed along different lines in Wallonia from those in Flanders since the state reform of 1970, which made the separate cultural communities in Belgium autonomous. Regulations about grants are not the same and neither are the qualifications required for the staff. In the Flemish community professional workers in the sector with university or higher vocational training which is relevant to this field may be paid from government funding, but people without these qualifications may only be admitted to this profession provided that they have several years of experience and follow an additional training course of either 120 or 240 hours. More details on these are included below. Altogether 500 to 600 people are involved each year and most of these work in associations and institutions.

THE MOST RELEVANT TRAINING COURSES

One would expect some attention to be paid to adult education in teacher training programmes for secondary school teaching at university and at the higher education level, considering the fact that adult education is gradually becoming the only sector to expand within the educational institution. But this is not the case. The subject of 'agogic' skills has only now been introduced to comply with the reforms in teacher training. But this only consists of learning how to handle children and their parents and how to function as a team.

Social pedagogics, or social agogy, is often provided at the faculties for pedagogic and psychological sciences at the universities. The problems surrounding adult education receive the most attention within the framework of this study, although it always occurs within the context of a broader study. Courses of this kind are organised at the Catholic University of Leuven, the Free University of Brussels and the state University of Ghent in Flanders. Thirty to fifty students graduate in this field each year.

The content of the courses varies from university to university; there are a number of compulsory subjects and also some optional ones. Of the compulsory ones some are more general and others are designed more specifically for the study of social pedagogics or social 'agogy'. The specific part of the courses consists of lectures, seminars, project work and in-service training. The course is completed by a major paper or essay.

The specific subjects include:

- social pedagogics (theory and practice)
- theories of 'agology' (community education/development)
- theory of neighbourhood work and community development/assistance/support
- planning and curriculum development
- methods and techniques
- group work
- the theory of organisations and systems
- government policy.

In addition, there are social academies, i.e. schools for social welfare and cultural work, community work and education. These have a long tradition in training staff for socio-cultural education. A three-year higher vocational training programme is provided within these institutions which prepares students for many professions in the social sector, including socio-cultural work. Graduates from these schools often end up in executive or other managerial positions, or as teachers in the field of social skills and social orientation.

The only specific training programme is the supplementary course which, in the first instance, is meant for people who lack the required qualifications but who wish to gain employment in a government-funded position. Additionally, this course is open to others who are interested in a systematic introduction to socio-cultural education. It may be regarded as the continuation of the Belgian-Dutch training programme for adult educators in non-formal education and development work which was established jointly between the two countries between 1965 and 1975. (This was the first training course for professional adult educators to be established in the Dutch-speaking part of Europe.) Since 1985 the course has been organised by the Flemish Centre for Adult Education (VCVO)[2] and lasts between 120 and 240 hours. It is now provided in modular form, i.e. blocks of six times forty (two times twenty) hours. The programme is as follows:

- knowledge of the field/statutory regulations,
- starting points, background requirements of socio-cultural preparation,
- working within organisations and institutions,
- group work,
- investigation into needs, curriculum development, evaluation,
- cultural policy.

In addition, participants are expected to produce a dissertation.

IN-SERVICE TRAINING

The main part of the adult educators' training course is incorporated into the organisations or institutions of adult education themselves. A distinction is made here between training and refresher training for professional, part-time and volunteer workers respectively.

Volunteers

Many volunteers are involved in socio-cultural development work as committee members. But in some kinds of work, such as literacy, i.e. adult basic education, they also lead groups. The organisations and institutions in which they are involved take the responsibility for the training and supervision of their workers and the content varies according to the nature and scope of their work. For instance, the training programme for literacy workers comprises:

- a general introduction to literacy work,
- co-leadership of a reading and writing group, these groups are always led by two people,
- regular exchange of experience between members of local teams,
- conferences and seminars.

This is provided by the professional staff or by the more

19

experienced leaders. Outside experts from, for instance, universities and secondary school teacher training institutions may be invited to participate.

Part-time adult educators

Although they form the largest group of workers in adult education they are rarely offered training or retraining courses. In the socio-cultural sector there is some guidance, but this is almost non-existent for posts in formal adult education or vocational training.

Professional adult educators

As stated above there are only a few professional workers in adult education and the majority of these are to be found in socio-cultural and vocational education for the unemployed. Some larger organisations provide an introductory course for new workers or send them on existing courses elsewhere.

The training institute (NCPOS) of the National Employment Service (RVA) trains tutors for their own vocational training for the unemployed. This is done partly individually on the job and, partly, collectively at the national centre. Basic training for new instructors lasts for between twenty and twenty-five days and the following subjects are covered:

- the organisation of vocational training,
- learning and the acquisition of knowledge and skills,
- curriculum development,
- evaluation,
- methods and techniques.

This centre also provides training courses for instructors in firms and service organisations. According to tradition, training in this field comprises a didactic/technical component on the one hand and training in communication skills on the other. In addition, the centre provides training courses for instructors from abroad, in co-operation with the central government. This takes place within the framework of bilateral agreements.

Particular points receiving attention in the last few years have been:

- expansion of the system of modules in vocational training

courses and the problems surrounding target-setting in short-term programmes,
* attitude training,
* training in social skills,
* video-led programmes.

THE OPEN PROVISION OF REFRESHER COURSES

A number of organisations and institutions in the Flemish community organise courses and training programmes relevant to adult education, without necessarily being intended especially for adult educators. Two kinds of training course, general and specific, are provided with the course content changing annually. The general training programmes include advanced training for social workers (approximately 1,500 hours in length) and a post-graduate masters degree in social welfare work. These courses last much longer and are more broadly based. The specific programmes include: working with audio-visual material, group work, role play, etc. People from the broad social welfare and formal education fields attend these, usually, short-term courses.

A BRIEF SUMMARY

Only a limited number of workers are engaged full-time in adult education and most of these have managerial and executive responsibilities in the sector, so that this explains why there are few specific training opportunities for them. There are many more volunteer and part-time workers than those employed full-time, which accounts for training at this level being built into the overall structure.

In recent years new forms of training have arisen for new fields of work and this applies particularly to adult basic education. Horizontal learning, i.e. learning from each other and teaching each other by sharing experiences, has become a focus for activities. However, there was, and still is, very little relevant knowledge at universities and institutions of higher education about this field generally.

It seems strange that little or no consideration is given to adult education in teacher training, and that particularly in formal adult education there is no form of further training at all. The only explanation for this is the absence of any coherent policy on adult education.

WHAT IS DESIRABLE?

It is obvious that the quality of adult education can be improved considerably through training and further training, and there is a real need for this since growth in the sector is expected to increase in years to come. Now the provision needs radical restructuring. For this reason it is safe to observe that the need for a sound training scheme for workers is greater than ever before. The first step towards this should be to lift the profile of adult education and thereby that of the adult educator.

A suitable model must be found in order to reach the large group of part-time and volunteer workers operating in the field. In the first instance, therefore, consideration within teacher training needs to be given to the problems surrounding adult education. The provision of a course, 'The Introduction to Adult Education', by the Open University would help but this is still a long way off. It would also contribute greatly to creating an image for adult education. Successful completion of this course could be made a compulsory requirement for admission to some posts.

Assuming that there is a common elementary provision it would seem best to split the training for professional staff into one stream for workers with managerial and executive responsibility and another for those whose main responsibility is teaching.

As tasks and functions in adult education are highly varied and the work fluctuates throughout the year, we do not feel justified in advocating a uniform provision but would indicate a need for a broad, varied and open provision, with well-prepared further training programmes and a variety of short courses. A systematic inventory of this provision, with a full course description, should also be made widely available. Such courses would benefit participants in their careers in adult education.

All this does not alter the fact that training should be integrated into the normal life of adult education organisations and institutions. It is desirable, therefore, to have these organisations implement a continuous policy of training and refresher training for their employees.

NOTES

1   Address: Viaductstraat 133, 1040 Brussels, Belgium.
2   Address: Visverkopersstraat 13, 1000 Brussels, Belgium.

3 Adult education in the Netherlands

Sanneke Bolhuis and Joke Wagenaar

This paper seeks to explore training and other ways of helping to develop expertise among workers in adult education in the Netherlands.

INTRODUCTION

Adult education in the Netherlands consists of a large variety of divergent kinds of education, grouped in different ways. Training will be discussed under the following sections: non-formal adult education and development work with adults, adult basic education, general secondary adult education, secondary vocational education, higher education for adults, correspondence courses and direct education provided by private bodies.

A detailed discussion of the many educational activities, institutions and types of worker is not possible within a single chapter, so that a number of specific activities, such as health education and guidance, education for child care and upbringing and staff training in recreational sports, are not included. Adult education through radio and television is mentioned, although the training and refresher courses for the various participants are not discussed below.

This chapter offers only a brief overview of the present situation. Each section opens with a brief description of the specific type of work and then goes on to discuss the training and other ways of developing expertise among the workers affected. Most sections provide a factual description, although in a number of instances plans for the near future will also be discussed. Finally, some general remarks are made.

Several developments will be discussed in the ensuing sections, but there are four current issues.

1 The General Act on Adult Education, the aim of which is to create coherence in, and further the development of, adult

education, has passed through parliament. Many items have to be settled, however, by legislation (enabling legislation) to put the Act into effect. The date on which this legislation will become effective has been delayed since the Act passed through parliament. However, on the strength of the General Act on Adult Education, a Council for Adult Education has been established. It is anticipated that as a result of the Act there will be educational planning at both local and state levels and a coherent support system, all of which will have a major effect on the present adult education provision. In addition, in anticipation of the enactment of the General Act on Adult Education the government grants scheme for basic education (see p. 28f) was put into operation.

There are also moves to change that part of the Act concerned with support services. The proposals in the Act for these services are pitched at three levels.

a   Local and regional educational centres should be mainly geared to giving information and advice to participants in the selection of subjects to study and also to ensuring coherence of provision and, in addition, they may offer workers in the service support and also indicate educational needs.

b   Authorities at provincial level should have the task of co-ordinating training and of initiating some curriculum development, as well as assisting with co-operation between educational centres.

c   A national agency should take note of, among other things, the training needs of the workers. It also indicates priorities with reference to a national support scheme laid down by the government.

The proposed scheme is a continuation of the development of adult education centres and provincial workshops which have been in operation for a number of years. However, major changes are still under discussion.

2   Higher vocational education in the Netherlands is now in a transitional phase. Vocational training programmes occupy a separate category in higher education in the Netherlands and have hardly any links with academic education at university level. This sector includes several types of vocational training, which are also of importance for workers in adult education, and which will be discussed on below. Moreover, further training for teachers is included in the statutory regulations for higher vocational education.

A new law for this form of education, as distinct from the General Act on Adult Education, became operative in

August 1986, in which statutory regulations and funding arrangements both have changed drastically. By and large, however, institutions will have a higher degree of autonomy in determining their own policies. At the same time a radical operation has been set in motion under the heading of 'Expansion, Division of Labour and Co-operation', which implies that several hundred separate schools are being re-organised into a few dozen large, multi-sectoral institutions, i.e. institutions operating vocational training programmes in various fields.

3   There is a great deal of discussion and planning about vocational education and training for young people and adults. Efforts are being made to develop a more coherent system, to fill the gaps in the provision and to make it more flexible in order to meet the rapidly changing needs of the labour market.

In the Netherlands much value is placed on vocational training as part of the educational system. The advantages of this include a broad qualification in which aspects of general education are included, as well as equal social status and greater ease of access. The lack of interaction with the labour market is, however, a drawback. This is why attempts are being made to find a new balance in sharing the obligations and in finding new ways to realise the joint responsibility of the government and employers' organisations and trades unions. Both trade and industry are starting to assume more responsibility again, i.e. they are investing more in vocational training and non-formal education of their employees.

It appears that somewhat more importance is being placed on the broader non-formal education and training of employees than is evident in purely job-specific training courses. An employee who is more flexible and more versatile is of great value in a rapidly changing branch of industry. In this respect the role of the trainer in trade and industry also becomes more significant. The provision of private institutions also comes more clearly into focus, as will be shown below.

4   Several efforts are being made to prepare the educational system to respond to the needs of the labour market. A new act allows schools to act as entrepreneurs, marketing courses and other aspects of their work. It is hoped, therefore, that through this they will forge closer links with the labour market and even with society as a whole. Second, a new Act on Vocational Education and Training is under discussion. The purpose of this legislation will be to improve the quality,

flexibility and efficiency of education and training for adults. Third, there is a variety of efforts being undertaken in the field of continuing education to make educational institutions and teachers much more 'market-minded'.

NON-FORMAL EDUCATION AND DEVELOPMENT WORK WITH ADULTS

Overview

Non-formal education and development work with adults aims at the promotion of personal development and social participation of persons and groups through learning and conscientisation processes. This work comprises a great diversity of activities: from language courses and courses directed to leisure activities to political development, emancipatory and action-directed activities. Non-formal education and development activities are not aimed at obtaining formal qualifications or diplomas. The work links up with the interest, experience and life situations of the (intended, targeted) groups of participants. There are, for instance, activities aimed at: emancipation and participation of women, ethnic minorities, elderly people, unemployed. Educational work with a particular target group is often part of a broader programme of supporting activities, so that the whole field may then be considered as a separate type of work, e.g. women's activities.

Non-formal education and development work are often characterised by a smooth transition to related activities (socio-cultural and community development work, library work, leisure time, cultural and religious activities and development of interests). Many institutes for non-formal education and development have participated in the expansion of adult basic education, which will be discussed separately in the next section.

Non-formal education and development work occur at residential adult education centres and folk high schools, local centres for liberal adult education, different organisations e.g. women's organisations and at community and neighbourhood centres — all of which have their own accommodation. In addition, this work is carried out by trades unions and organisations for ethnic minority groups. These different organisations all have their own traditions and focus upon specific kinds of activities, target groups and workers. Some institutions work exclusively with a professional staff, while others have a mainly or partly volunteer staff. Visiting lecturers are also employed in many cases.

Finally, educational radio and television programmes are often aimed at similar types of person as are the non-formal education and development courses.

Training and other ways of developing expertise in non-formal adult education

Traditionally, we can speak of non-formal adult education as being an 'open profession' in the Netherlands, i.e. the work undertaken is not dependent upon one particular type of training. People with highly diverse preliminary training and experience have found employment in non-formal adult education and development work. For this variety of recruitment there is a diversified provision of in-service training programmes, which are mostly of a brief and part-time nature. Trained workers as well as volunteers without vocational training make use of this provision.

Training for non-formal education and development work is offered by post-secondary institutions for higher vocational education, which provide full-time and part-time courses in social, cultural, personal and institutional work as well as in community development. The departments of cultural work in particular focus upon educational aspects of working with adults. The emphasis given to education has been increasing over the past few years and several schools are giving students the opportunity to specialise in adult education. This specialisation may cover a short course of a few months or it may span as long as a three-year study period.

Second, university graduates in andragogy can work as professionals in non-formal education and development work, particularly in support functions and also in staff development roles. Adult education is one of the disciplines within andragogy.

The remaining non-formal education and development work is undertaken by workers from a variety of training backgrounds, including, for example, teacher training colleges for primary, secondary and university education with such specialisms as theology, agriculture, economics, law and sociology.

Additionally, as was mentioned earlier, provision is made for refresher training for both professionals and volunteers. This provision includes introduction or supervision of new workers, seminars and workshops for executive and co-ordinating officers, courses, i.e. seminars and workshops, for those working with specific groups, specific subjects and educational materials

27

and methods. The different types of training, and the extent to which use is made of them, vary according to institutions and individuals. Large institutions offer the provision, either independently or in co-operation with other institutions in the region and, on occasions, in co-operation with national organisations. The latter have staffs with specific training functions. In addition, institutes for higher vocational education are becoming increasingly involved in training for the non-formal educational field.

Organisations working exclusively with volunteers, e.g. women's groups, make use of local residential adult education courses of training. Provincial educational workshops contribute to the training activities.

In the past few years several courses for adult education have been included in the provision of further training carried out by teacher training institutions under the jurisdiction of the Ministry of Education. In this context it should be emphasised that this is open to all those people working within the field of adult education, even if they do not possess a formal teaching qualification.

Finally, there are advanced 'agogic' training courses for professionals with higher vocational education and a few years of practical experience. Among other specialist options in this advanced training programme is one in adult education. The training programme consists of a two-year, part-time course leading to an extension of the professional qualification and to a first-grade teaching qualification in the relevant subjects. The issue of teaching qualifications is discussed more fully later in the chapter.

ADULT BASIC EDUCATION

Overview

In the past ten to fifteen years educational activities have been developed throughout the country for those who have had little formal education. The question as to which activities should be included within basic education is directly linked to the question as to which activities are related to government funding. These activities are, to a large extent, developed at the initiative of individuals in various fields, e.g. schools, social work, neighbourhood centres, local adult education centres.

The central government contributed to this development by setting up the Open School pilot projects between 1977 and 1980 in fourteen different localities. These were educational provisions for adults with at most two years' secondary education, but it was also discovered that there were many other adults who had had even less education. Since 1980 the central government has continued to provide grants for the following developmental projects: literacy activities, educational activities for cultural minorities, introduction of the Open School method, i.e. a continuation of the Open School by different co-operating adult educational institutions, and co-operative projects in vocational education.

Radio and television was used for the Open School pilot projects. Since then the educational radio and television programmes have been produced for various target groups in adult basic education. The State Regulation for Adult Basic Education became effective in 1986 and was operationalised during 1987. According to these regulations, adult basic education activities are directed towards:

1 The acquisition of skills — (i) Language skills: a basic ability to use the Dutch language in both personal and social life in both its oral and written forms. Inhabitants of the province of Friesland may also acquire Friesian-language skills. Illiterates from ethnic minorities have opportunity to learn enough of their own language to enable them to learn Dutch. Additionally, the opportunity to learn some English is available. (ii) Numerical skills: the ability to use the basic principles of arithmetic in personal and social life. (iii) Social skills: the ability to use knowledge and insight in personal and social life.
2 Guidance and access to secondary education or other social activities.
3 Outreach, recruitment and guidance in adult basic education.

The debate about precisely which elements are to be covered by the State Regulation has not yet ended and this is due, in part, to the fact that there is only a limited budget available. The State Regulation aims at professionalisation of adult basic education, which should be the province of professional workers who have the required expertise. However, because of the lack of financial resources volunteers still have an important role to play in basic education.

Training and other ways of promoting expertise among adult basic educators

In the past years professional workers, many volunteers and even semi-volunteers have been involved in adult basic education. Quite a few have received a training which is more or less suited to this work, e.g. at teacher training colleges in primary or secondary education, at higher vocational institutes for mainly social, cultural and community work, etc. Others have had only practical experience in the situations in which they have worked. Some workers from ethnic minority groups have formal educational qualifications from their native countries, some have secondary or higher education, some are secondary school dropouts but many are deficient in their own knowledge of the Dutch language and society.

The development of adult basic education has gone hand in hand with a large number of diverse activities promoting training for both paid and volunteer workers. The content and approaches were nearly always restricted to one of the adult basic education activities and target groups. Most activities were necessarily limited in scope. Most of the staff work part-time in adult basic education and financial resources for training have always been limited. The extent to which workers participate in training activities varies greatly, as does the experience of the participants which means that the training itself is extremely diverse in accordance with the participant groups' needs.

A future training programme

In view of the professionalisation of adult basic education a crash training programme has been introduced to give the present workers an opportunity, where necessary, to extend their skills. This programme is modular in design so that each module can be studied separately. The programme consists of both general subjects (objectives, functions, target groups, adult learning and adult basic educational curriculum, group work, counselling and guidance, etc.) and of parts geared specifically to adult basic education (Dutch as first and second language, arithmetic, social skills, etc.). In addition, a crash course for ethnic workers has been started. The subjects mentioned above were used at the same time as a further training programme. In addition, a training programme for co-ordinators of basic education has been introduced. This crash training programme is designed to serve as the first phase in the development of regular training and further training for adult basic education workers. All of this training falls under the heading of higher vocational education, which was discussed earlier in the chapter.

The basic education programme can become the first vocational training programme specifically geared to one form of adult education. Parts of the programme (with necessary adjustments) can be useful for the training of other groups of adult educators as well. This is possible in the form of further training courses, but also through the incorporation of particular elements in the teacher training programmes. Another possibility is a vocational training programme for adult educators, but the several alternatives are still under discussion.

GENERAL SECONDARY EDUCATION FOR ADULTS

Overview

General secondary education for adults is, broadly speaking, similar to youth education and, by the same token, policy making in this sector is the responsibility of the Ministry of Education and Science. General secondary adult education offers part-time diploma courses in: 1) junior (the lowest level of) general secondary education (mavo); 2) senior general secondary education (havo); 3) pre-university education (vwo). With the diplomas earned, successful candidates can enter: 1) the higher level of secondary education (general and vocational); 2) higher vocational education; 3) university education.

Courses are offered in adult education schools both during the day and in the evening. Participants can take the five or six subjects necessary for the examination or confine themselves to working for separate certificates which can be used towards the award of the diploma. This form of adult education is spread widely throughout the country.

In the past a large number of teachers were teaching a few hours a week in adult education in addition to their full-time jobs in youth education. However, since 1981 government policy has been directed towards preventing overtime. Through this policy adult education teachers now have more teaching hours and confine themselves to one job. This has contributed to the teachers themselves regarding adult education as a more independent sector.

Training and further training

There are now two levels of qualification for teachers in general secondary adult education, each referring to the level of education for which the teaching qualification is valid. Teachers are trained at:

1 higher vocational institutes, where they can earn a second-grade qualification through full-time or part-time courses;
2 universities where a secondary-school first-grade teaching qualification may be obtained, linked with a university degree.

These training programmes generally pay little or no attention to adult education, although there has been an increasing interest in this field in the past few years.

Teachers in both youth and adult education may take advantage of extensive further training provision being offered by various teacher training institutes, although they are not compelled to do so. The subjects for the further training courses are no longer totally determined by the central government. The educational institutes may spend a proportion of their budget for further staff training according to their own local needs. Until now only a few courses have been specifically related to teaching adults or deal with specific forms of work and organisation in formal adult education settings, an example of this is the topic 'working with modular programmes'.

Further training programmes can be followed individually or with the school team, the team approach being on the increase. Staff-centred further education has the advantage that it is possible to concentrate upon certain practical problems and that the chance of introducing new methods is greater than when there are only a few teachers following the course. In addition, it will be recalled from an earlier section that further training courses for adult educators are also accessible for those who do not have a teaching diploma.

SECONDARY VOCATIONAL EDUCATION

Overview

The field of secondary vocational education and training is complicated for several reasons. First, there are a number of training institutes for unemployed adults and these are directly connected with the manpower services. Second, there is an apprenticeship system which was established for young people, but which is being made available to adults. Third, there are institutes offering part-time vocational courses that are equivalent to the full-time ones for young people. Fourth, many of the projects and activities which have been started in order to improve vocational education and training have been especially designed for different clientele, e.g. the poorly educated, ethnic groups, women etc. In addition, as was pointed out previously, new legislation is currently being considered.

Skill centres for adults (CVVs)

These were established in 1945 in order to match supply and demand in the labour market. These centres offer re-training and refresher courses for job seekers, following a method developed in Switzerland for individual intensive training programmes using centrally produced lesson material. The course participants acquire a vocation through self-study and the completion of exercises based upon written assignments. Instructors function mainly as resource persons, although they do demonstrate certain technical skills that cannot be explained in written form. In addition, they assess the students' (written) work. There are various courses in construction and metal work, and courses in clerical/office work, including information technology. In the past only full-time courses were offered but recently a number of part-time courses have been commenced. All of these courses last between four and twenty months and they are highly geared to professional practice.

Centres for vocational guidance and professional practice (CBBs)

These were established in 1978 and have been geared to the concerns of job seekers who, because of social and cultural reasons, have had little chance of employment. Cultural minorities form an important target group. The centres offer opportunities to acquire knowledge and skills necessary for employment or even those necessary to be accepted into a training programme. The total time available both for orientation and work experience is about one year. CBBs offer a few possibilities for part-time study. Both the CBBs and the CVVs are the responsibility of the Ministry of Social Affairs and

Employment, but they will become part of the shared responsibility that was discussed above.

Apprenticeship

The apprenticeship system consists of about 350 vocational training programmes in such areas as the technological services, industry, the hotel industry, bakeries, hairdressing, business and clerical spheres. These are open to young people, sixteen years and above, and also to adults of all ages. The theoretical instruction in these areas is provided by day-release education, one day each week, in the regional vocational schools. On the remaining four days the trainees receive practical training in firms and other business organisations under the supervision of instructors. Admission to these schemes is restricted to those who have already achieved either a junior-secondary general or junior-secondary vocational education.

Apprenticeship includes a basic training of (minimally) two years for which trades certificates are awarded. Thereafter, it is possible to opt for advanced training which lasts for another one or two years. For older trainees there are many short courses, e.g. a series of sixteen evening courses offered at these regional vocational schools.

Since 1983, projects have been developed in primary vocational education aiming at improving educational provision for women with a low level of training, for cultural minorities, for the unemployed and for those being threatened with unemployment. The participants can follow a training programme which may last from between several months to three years depending upon the opportunities of the labour market. Institutions for formal vocational education, non-formal education and general secondary education participate in these projects. Besides the vocational qualification aspect, vocational orientation and general education are also provided.

In addition, courses have been developed for women who have been out of employment for a long time, ('return to work' courses, fresh horizons, etc). These are offered by various institutions falling within the areas of policy of different ministries. They are geared to vocational orientation and/or professional practice — especially in technical subjects. Special vocational schools for women were also initiated by the Women's Union (of the Federation of Dutch Trades' Unions). These schools offer courses in information technology, 'start your own business' courses, and other forms of training.

Finally, a word about senior-secondary vocational education, where once again the opportunities for adults are much more limited than for youngsters. Only clerical/office studies can be taken in an institution which is especially orientated to adults. Other forms of senior-vocational secondary education, i.e. technical education, laboratory technicians' courses, socio-pedagogical and agricultural education make part-time provision for adults. There are also various refresher courses offered in both the agricultural and horticultural sectors, with lessons being conducted in the evenings by teachers from the day schools.

Training and refresher courses for tutors

Just as in general secondary education, tutors teaching adults in the above-mentioned programmes have been trained to teach in the youth education system in different secondary teacher training institutions or at universities. Exceptions to this rule are the instructors in the Adult Skill Centres.

Tutors in vocational education teach either general or vocational subjects. The general subjects correspond to those taught in general secondary education. For a number of vocational subjects it is possible to take a secondary teacher training course part time. For yet other subjects there is no secondary teacher training offered, although in these cases there are further training courses available for people working in the profession concerned, e.g. hairdressing. These courses are arranged by committees representing the trades involved, and they also assist in the development of vocational training programmes.

Further training provision for tutors in formal vocational education corresponds partly to the provision made for the tutors in general secondary education. It is highly diverse, being geared to the occupation and the subject matter, as well as to the more general aspects, such as organisation, student counselling, etc. Very few courses are directly related to teaching adults in formal vocational education and those that are come under the responsibility of the Ministries of Education and Science and of Agriculture and Fisheries; these are conducted by various training institutes for secondary school teachers. The further training provision for tutors in agricultural education includes several courses of study expressly aimed at organisers of adult courses and tutors.

A general problem is that only part of the further education provision can be realised because of the lack of participants;

tutors have too little time and do not receive educational leave to undertake further training and yet this is supposed to be an element in the support structure.

At the Skill Centres for Adults instructors are appointed for their working experience and competence in the area in which they are to give instruction. Over the years it has become evident that some initial didactical training for instructors is desirable. For those who are just beginning there is a short course. Although the instructors are not obliged to attend the course, they usually do so. Some of them also take a two-year course for teacher practitioners as discussed on p. 28. Apart from this more general refresher course, there is also refresher training in each of the occupations, offered in subjects of which the older instructors might not have had any experience, e.g. mass production methods in the building trade.

At the CBBs, most of the tutors have an officially recognised teaching qualification. Apart from incidental seminars there is no further education provision especially geared to the work. Because so many foreign workers are registered at these centres, tutors tend to use the further training provision that is offered for educators working with these people. Further training may also result from contacts made through arranging placements; for instance, automation in firms where trainees have been placed has led to tutors taking courses in information technology, so that they can keep up with developments in trade and industry.

HIGHER EDUCATION FOR ADULTS

Overview

Included within adult education is that part of higher vocational education which is provided on a part-time basis, i.e. aimed at those who seek to combine their studies with their work and/or other tasks, such as housekeeping or raising a family. These studies do not attend immediately after leaving the secondary education system. Higher vocational education comprises quite a few part-time courses, followed by some 25 per cent of the students, in such areas as technology, pedagogy, health and art education, librarianship and teaching. The courses are concentrated into two or three days a week, several days a month, or evenings; bedsides this there are a number of separate adult evening (night) schools offering business courses. These courses take between two and five years. Developments in higher vocational education, as indicated above, will perhaps lead to the creation of more educational opportunities for adults in the future.

Universities

These have recently started to offer part-time training (especially evening courses) in a rather broader area than previously. Part-time studies take a little longer than normal courses and the increase in this provision can be partly explained by the decrease in student population because of both demographic factors and new legislation on university education which restricts the length of study to a maximum of six years. By offering part-time provision the universities are aiming at a growing market of people who wish to combine work and family responsibilities and studies. More recently the elderly have constituted a new target group for the universities, which have begun to offer special courses for them. Adults also enrol with the Open University, which started in 1984 and offers tuition by correspondence in law, economics and industrial and administrative science, and in technical, natural, cultural and social sciences. In these cases, adequate previous knowledge is presumed, but formal qualifications are not a prerequisite for following a course. The prepared study pack of modules, which may be followed at the students' own learning pace, may be put together in such a way as to form an equivalency to one in normal higher education. There are eighteen study centres throughout the country, where Open University students can obtain advice, counselling and take their examinations.

Training and further training for tutors

Tutors in higher vocational education are required to have a first-grade teaching certificate. Further education is aimed at such aspects as working models and educational skills with, for instance, attention being paid to modular courses and new fields of learning. Further training of tutors in this area does not usually refer to the teaching of adults. Other themes in further education provision are concerned with knowledge and skills to deal with processes of change and amalgamation.

University tutors may, to a certain extent, participate in courses for the improvement of didactics, organisation or the content of courses. Themes involved here do not concern the specific field of part-time adult formal education, but rather such aspects as project education (research), project management and information technology. Tutors are also expected to keep abreast of developments in their own profession and thereby make an active contribution to this. Open University tutors first take courses in the areas which are new to them, such as 'distance learning' and 'working with older students' and the content of such courses is geared to the needs of the team responsible for drawing up the particular study programme.

PRIVATE CORRESPONDENCE AND DIRECT EDUCATION

Overview

Correspondence courses, available as early as the nineteenth century in the Netherlands, have always been a significant form of adult education. Approximately 70 per cent of all of these courses are vocational in nature, some leading to official state qualifications.

Instruction is no longer exclusively presented on the basis of written material. Currently it is frequently supplemented by audio-cassettes, practicals and face-to-face tuition. Institutions offering correspondence education may apply for accreditation. Until 1987, it was possible for them to do this according to the act on accreditation for institutions offering correspondence tuition (WEISO) of 1973. Approximately half of the correspondence education on offer is officially recognised.

Another very extensive sector of adult education comprises private institutions and organisations offering face-to-face tuition. There is a great variety both of courses and institutions and a significant part of this provision is vocationally orientated. For instance, there are many clerical/office work and information technology courses. In 1987, the 1973 Accreditation Act was replaced by a Law on Accreditation for Educational Institutions and this will also accommodate these private institutions offering direct forms of education.

The training programmes preparing candidates for examinations which lead to qualifications needed for self-employment, such as those of the textile and hotel and catering industries, are a special category, and they are subject to the inspection of the Ministry of Economic Affairs. About a dozen organisations offer courses of this nature, on a part-time basis and usually in the evenings. Legislation is in preparation to arrange for the partial funding of these courses by government (the new Act on Vocational Education and Training which was mentioned in the introduction to this chapter).

On-the-job training is also a form of direct education. Most companies either entrust their training to outside institutions, or conduct their own training again, or utilise a combination of both. Increased automation in industry, causing a rapid change in job profiles, is an important contributory factor in this development. The government stimulates trade and industry to offer training to its own employees by providing financial support. Sometime the government partly funds special initiatives on a temporary basis.

Training and refresher training for tutors

On the basis of WEISO, the government provides accreditation to institutions meeting certain criteria, including the relevance of the content of the course and the provision of student guidance by the institution. Additionally, the qualifications of the writers and tutors of such courses are taken into consideration in this accreditation exercise. Authors and tutors of programmes leading to a state examination should hold appropriate teaching qualifications. The accredited institutions are expected to determine the level of desired qualifications of the other authors and tutors in consultation with the inspectorate for correspondence education.

The trainers in firms and institutions, such as health organisations, may participate in the mainly vocational training offered by various branches of industry or by other large firms and organisations. Furthermore, they may also take part in training courses for instructors, which are now provided by the renewed and extended higher vocational institute, the Pedagogical Technical High School. Courses, varying from a few days to a two-year programme, are aimed, above all, at pedagogical/didactical expertise. The participant trainers may work in any sector: the industrial and business sectors as well as banking, nursing, chain stores, etc.

The subject matter of this training programme for instructors is presented in study packs and participants are expected, among other things, to indicate in their assignments what they would like to change in their work. For second-year students there are various choices, one of which is 'Teaching Adults'. The study packs concerned with this option are focused on adult learning, methods of teaching adults and different perspectives on policy. The course is recognised by the Ministry of Education and Science, i.e. the Ministry guarantees continuity, quality and funding. There is no official examination but a credit system exists (each study pack has a credit award) and a diploma is awarded if the minimum number of credits is obtained.

GENERAL COMMENTS

Surveying the highly diverse field of adult education leads to the conclusion that the training of most adult educators is not at all, or only partially, geared to working with adults. In the area of further training for adult educators there are opportunities in some sectors but in others hardly any exist. However, it must be noted that greater initiatives are being taken at the present time than in the past. There is a slowly developing trend of professionalisation in adult education which is beginning to be seen as a separate field with characteristics of its own. The idea that a different approach is required in the education of adults corresponds to similar trends in youth education. Teacher training programmes have in the past decade been continuing to shift the emphasis, no longer only on course content but also on didactical aspects and pedagogical guidance in a more integrated manner. These training courses have therefore become more age-group related and therefore linked to the specific type of educational institution.

The extent to which, and the manner in which, course content is related to didactical and agogic aspects still requires a great deal of attention. This applies to different forms of adult education as well as to further training and development of expertise. Both the needs of the target groups and the type of educational activity are important. In this way, for example, it will be essential for target groups to be offered a combination of subject-orientated course content and counselling. The focus on the subject matter is often strongest in vocational education and this has been greatly emphasised because of the necessary changes in it due to rapid technological developments. On the other hand, the effectiveness of training will be greatly increased if the approach is actually geared to the target groups.

In view of the large number of workers in adult education, their further training will, for the time being, be at least as important as creating initial vocational training programmes for adult education. An advantage in further training is that it provides an opportunity to build on the experience of the participants so that the theory and practice may interact. There is, however, a reluctance to participate in further training because of lack of time and because there is little obligation to do so. Further training should be included more often in a tutor's job description and in institutional planning. The more new initiatives and/or activities that have been undertaken for other target groups, the more the need of further training is felt. There is an increasing provision for this in such areas as basic adult education. In the new system on legal status and salaries in education, further training is compulsory for promotion, although only to a limited extent.

In different forms of training for teachers, e.g. socio-cultural workers, school teachers, etc., adult education is beginning to gain ground. This is partly due to the reduction of job opportunities in the youth education system because of demographic changes. The new structure of higher vocational education, in which larger entities are created and where institutions have more autonomy, as was discussed above, offers more opportunities for the inclusion of adult education, both in the basic programmes and in further training programmes. It is of fundamental importance that the training institutions create and maintain a close relationship with the field of adult education and support agencies. All three are in a developmental stage and they can only grow in a meaningful way if they are successful in maintaining continuous interaction with each other.

BIBLIOGRAPHY

Bolhuis, S.M. (1989) *Vormen van volwasseneneducatie. Een verkenning anno 1988*, Gids Volwasseneneducatie.

Fordham, P.E. and Fox, J. (1989) 'Training the adult educator as a professional', *International Review of Education*, vol. 35, no. 2.

Adult Education in the Netherlands (1986) NCVO Department of International Relations, PO Box 351, 3800 AJ Amersfoort, The Netherlands. (A loose-leaf collection of essays by a variety of authors giving an overall impression of adult education in the Netherlands.)

Teaching Staff in Dutch Vocational Education (1983) Berlin: CEDEFOP.

The Training and Further Training of Adult Educators (1982) Report of the Geiranger Conference, European Bureau of Adult Education, PO Box 367, 3800 AJ Amersfoort, The Netherlands. (Report on the Netherlands included within these conference papers.)

Naar professionalisering van de werkers in de basiseducatie (1986) Den Haag: Programma-commissie Deskundigheid Basiseducatie.

Part II

English-speaking countries

4 Adult education in the Republic of Ireland: The training of adult educators

Declan G. Irvine

INTRODUCTION

The report *Adult Education in Ireland* (1973, 3.3.8) recommended that 'the training of adult educators and community development workers be considered as a vital, urgent and necessary element in the national provision of adult education'. Eleven years later, the second national report on adult education in Ireland (*Lifelong Learning* 1984: 5.2.) re-echoed these sentiments, when it recommended that 'appropriate levels of initial and inservice training of adult educators be ensured at both national and local levels'. One might be forgiven for assuming that the need for the formal education and training of those involved in adult education is particularly acute in, or even exclusive to Ireland, based on the comments of the aforementioned reports. However, evidence from other countries, some much more developed than Ireland, suggests that training, both initial and in-service is a serious issue worldwide — as is instanced by the chapters in this volume. For example, delegates from 122 countries to the fourth UNESCO International Conference on Adult Education in 1985 cited the mobilisation and training of sufficient personnel as the 'biggest challenge facing the field' (UNESCO 1985). In spite of the widespread acceptance of adult education as an essential instrument for socio-economic and cultural health (Boshier 1985: 3) why has the professionalisation of adult education, which has as a basic requirement the initial and in-service training of personnel, been so slow to develop? Even in North American where there has been an explosive growth in the numbers participating in adult education, little has changed over the last twenty years regarding the training of adult educators (Hartman 1983/4). Is this simply a situation where the 'Cinderella' status of adult education (Russell Report 1973) is in great part due to the lack of professionalism among its personnel, or is the latter the cause of the low status or marginality of adult education? This alleged marginality of adult education, or its status or role, not only in relationship to the educational system of a country

45

but to the social structure of any society, is probably the key to any understanding of the provision of training for adult educators in any given society.

Another factor which complicates the issue is the distinction between the 'missionary' and the 'professional' functions of the educator of adults. Is the gifted enthusiast rather than the knowledgeable and skilful person more likely to succeed as a tutor of adults? The Murphy Report (1973), Boshier (1985) and Legge (1985) refer to the doubt, which exists in the minds of many people from different backgrounds and cultures, as to whether the training of adult educators is either useful or necessary. *Experientia docet* is the practice, if not indeed the principle, which governs issues relating to the training of adult educators in many countries. Legge (1985: 59) sums up this view very aptly when he states that 'the long established opinion that a teacher of adults only needs subject knowledge, and the planner or administrator only common sense and office skills, dies hard, as does the view that training for competence in the adult education sector is impossible and, if possible, then highly undesirable.' As a consequence of the above-mentioned attitudes, it is hardly any wonder that the training of adult educators is, in many countries, sketchy, narrow and a patchwork of piecemeal offerings, rather than an integrated part of the professional development of adult educators.

Any attempt, therefore, to understand provision for the training of adult educators in a country must incorporate an examination of the place and status of adult education within it; its historical development and its relationship, not only to full-time education provision, but also to other institutions in the country concerned.

EDUCATION IN IRELAND

According to the provisional statistics of the 1986 census of Ireland, there are approximately 3.5 million people in the Irish Republic. The country has, in relation to developed countries generally, one of the highest dependency ratios — namely 70 per cent. This massive ratio can be understood when one examines the structure of the Irish population. Almost one-half of the total population is under twenty-five years of age, while some 30 per cent are under the age of sixteen. A very approximate additional division of the population structure illuminates the scene further: almost one-third of people in Ireland are in full-time education; another third are in employment and the remainder are, for various reasons, not in work. The birth rate has shown some signs of decline since 1981 and the effects of this are only now being seen in the participation rates in the early years of schooling. Almost 40 per cent of the population dwell in rural areas, although urbanisation and internal migration have led, generally, to a decline in the smaller centres and an increase in the number of people living in larger concentrations of population. The age range for compulsory schooling is from six to fifteen years, although almost half of the four-and five-year-olds also attend primary schools. Fifty-two per cent of those between fifteen and eighteen years are now in full-time education while, in recent years, only approximately 10 per cent of those over twenty are in full-time education. Approximately 60 per cent of those in full-time education attend primary schools, about 30 per cent attend secondary schools and 5 per cent participate in the third level of education. Since the 1960s, all children have the right to free education in the first and second levels and scholarships are available to approximately 40 per cent of those who participate in third-level education.

Like many countries, Ireland has experienced an 'explosion' in the numbers participating in full-time education. For example, the number engaged in second-level education has doubled over the last twenty years or so. Competitiveness, based upon a meritocratic view of society and education, has increased, due to the fact that in Ireland, as elsewhere, education is viewed as a major vehicle for social mobility and a substitute for family background and inherited wealth. The recent economic recession has contributed significantly to the pattern of extended schooling, whereby schools increasingly perform 'holding operations' in the hope of an improved economic climate and more occupational opportunities becoming available. While many efforts have been made to achieve equality of opportunity in education, factors such as social class, participation rates in second-level education, and distance from educational establishments continue to restrict the chances of a large proportion of the population from furthering their eduction, especially at the third level (Clancy 1982). Inflation has also had its effects, and fees at third-level institutions in Ireland have doubled over the last few years.

ADULT EDUCATION IN IRELAND: AN HISTORICAL OVERVIEW

A brief historical overview of the development of adult

education in Ireland is necessary if one is to attempt to understand its present status. The position of adult education within Irish society generally, and its relationship to the total education system will, to a significant extent, determine the nature and extent of training for adult educators.

The Kenny Report (1984: IV.2) states the present position very clearly:

> Adult education is not at present an administratively distinct sector of the educational system. There is a diversity of agencies. They include the formal institutions of second and third level education as well as a variety of statutory and voluntary bodies and community groups. The statutory agencies operate under a number of government departments. The voluntary agencies which are state-aided, are aided to different degrees and from a variety of government funds.

Not only is there great diversity among the providers of adult education in Ireland, there also exists an extensive range of courses, varying in content, duration and demands made on the participants. 'One of the results of this variety, with differences in organisational structures, objectives and clientele, is their lack of identity as adult education agencies' (Murphy 1973: 2.3.1.). Such a patternless mosaic of activities, complicated further by the fact that the vast majority of those working in adult education do so in a part-time capacity only, contributes to the 'invisibility' of adult education as a professional enterprise and to its status relative to other forms and systems of education. According to O'Murchu (1984: 23) 'this variety of adult education services can be attributed as much to the historical evolution over more than two hundred and fifty years, as to the appearance in recent decades of organisations and agencies catering specifically for certain categories.'

Adult education, in the non-populist sense, dates from the founding of the Royal Dublin Society in 1731. This organisation, although mainly catering for the upper or relatively wealthy classes, through its education activities, sowed the seeds of many adult education enterprises today. Education for a much wider clientele, namely trades people and artisans, was provided by Mechanics' Institutes from 1825, and contributed towards the provision of public libraries from the middle of the last century onwards. National organisations, such as the Gaelic Athletic Association and the Gaelic League, began their work for the betterment of the people of Ireland in the last decade of the Nineteenth century. The growth of co-operatives, especially the

Irish Agricultural Organisation Society, led to the establishment in 1900 of the Departments of Agriculture and Technical Instruction, whose brief included not only the education and training of farmers, but also the training of teachers and instructors to carry out its work in rural areas. The United Irishwomen's Association, the predecessor of the foremost women's organisation in Ireland today, the Irish Countrywomen's Association, also dates from this period.

Major developments of significance to adult education have also occurred during the past fifty years. A combination of legislation, i.e. the 1930 Vocational Education Act, the 1931 Agricultural Act, and the growth of organisations in rural areas, i.e. Muintir na Tire (1939), Young Farmers (1940), Macra na Feirme (1944), Macra na Tuaithe (1951), the National Farmers Association (1955), have all contributed to the greater provision of adult education by statutory and voluntary bodies. The development of university extra-mural programmes in the 1940s, the introduction of part-time (evening) degree courses and the establishment of voluntary and non-voluntary colleges for adult education, such as the People's College (1948), the Dublin Institute of Adult Education (1950) and the College of Industrial Relations (1951), added a further dimension to an already multi-faceted system of adult education (O'Murchu 1984: chapter 3).

The first national report, *Adult Education in Ireland*, was published in 1973, and a second report, *Lifelong Learning*, followed in 1984. These publications and the spirit which promoted their proposed execution, would seem to indicate that adult education was eventually to receive the recognition that it deserved. Unfortunately this was not to be so. Some recommendations of the Murphy Report (1973) were implemented, in a rather piecemeal fashion, but as yet the major thrust of both reports, i.e. the recognition of adult education as an integral part of the total educational provision and the establishment of a structure (national, local and statutory) to facilitate provision and development, has not even been attempted. Recognition, in the form of substantial financial aid, was only recently granted to Aontas — the national association for adult education in Ireland.

Three other independent reports *An Award Structure for Recurrent Education* (1978), *Towards Facilitating Awards in Adult and Continuing Education* (1985), and *Extending Educational Opportunity Through NCEA Awards by Distance Learning* (1985) were all commissioned by the National Council for Educational Awards (the national developmental and monitoring body for technical, industrial, scientific, technological, commercial and art education, outside the universities). They provide further indications of deeply held convictions that adult education in Ireland is becoming a priority area for development.

ADULT EDUCATION IN IRELAND TODAY

> Adult education in Ireland resembles a mosaic of initiatives and motivations, ideas and idealism, objectives and programmes with a solid foundation originally in the voluntary, non-statutory, sector, later strengthened by the state and statutory sector. The cumulative result is the provision of adult education services which are organisationally and structurally far from simple or uncomplicated.
>
> (O'Murchu 1984: 56)

This is a very accurate description of the state of adult education in Ireland today. The work of Schroeder (1970) distinguishes four different types of provider:

1 Agencies whose central function is adult education, e.g. colleges of adult education.
2 Agencies whose main function is youth education and who have adult education as an added responsibility (adult education as a secondary function), e.g. universities, colleges of higher education, schools.
3 Agencies which have educational and non-educational roles and use adult education to fulfil some of their responsibilities (adult education as an allied function), e.g. libraries, museums, health, welfare organisations.
4 Agencies which serve special interest groups and which use adult education for specific purposes only (adult education as a subordinate function), e.g. trades unions, churches, government agencies, voluntary bodies.

Boshier's (1985: 6) comment that few agencies have adult education as a central function and that in most instances it is a 'secondary', 'allied' or 'subordinate' function, is a valid one for Ireland today. Fourteen government departments have some responsibility for adult education and many of them financial or administrative roles only. The Departments of Education and Agriculture play more direct roles in the actual provision of educational programmes for adults through their own agencies.

Institutes of formal education in Ireland vary significantly in their respective contributions to adult education. Little evidence exists of involvement in the education of adults by the various agencies of elementary education. Secondary schools, which are mainly voluntary schools and run by religious orders, have only recently become involved. Comprehensive and community schools are more actively engaged in adult education and have directors of adult education in post whose responsibility it is to promote and provide adult education in their respective catchment areas.

The major providers of adult education in Ireland are the Vocational Education Committees which were established by the Vocational Education Act of 1930. These committees provide formal second-level education for young people in their areas and also interpret the term 'continuing education' as used in Section 3 of the 1930 Act as their mandate for the provision of adult education. Until the 1960s, the courses provided were generally of a trade, secretarial or hobby nature. In recent years, however, a much more comprehensive range of courses has been offered. Vocational Education Committees employ over 5,000 full-time second-level teachers, and over 6,000 part-time teachers who work mainly in the adult education sector. Annually, over five million hours of tuition are provided to over 150,000 adults in over 1,000 subjects (IVEA 1986). In recent years, the number of students on part-time courses was almost double the number of those on full-time courses, suggesting a trend towards increased provision for those beyond the age of compulsory schooling (adults). Based on a recommendation of the Murphy Report (1973), fifty full-time adult education organisers were appointed by the Vocational Education Committees in 1979; their roles include the identification and servicing of the educational needs of adults in their areas.

Each of the universities also provides some form of education for adults, normally through their extra-mural departments. Within the university system, full-time adult education officers organise learning opportunities for adults in their catchment areas. Courses range from short eight-week non-credit courses to two- and three-year certificate, diploma, degree and post-graduate part-time courses. Only a few full-time teaching staff are employed in adult education provision by the universities; however, there is a growing involvement, in a part-time capacity, of full-time university personnel in adult education. This contrasts with the pattern in Britain where full-time university staff are normally appointed as adult educators. However, the system in Ireland which may seem inferior to the

British provision, in relation to the full-time staff in adult education, has a very definite advantage in that university courses are serviced by staff from representative fields in the whole university, rather than by staff from a single department. Over the last few years the number of 'adult' students attending universities and other third-level institutions has increased very significantly. Extra-mural departments work closely with Vocational Education Committees, statutory bodies and national and local voluntary groups in offering educational programmes for many categories of adult.

Other third-level institutions, such as the national institutes for higher education, the National College for Art and Design, the Dublin Institute of Technology and the regional technical colleges also offer wide-ranging courses for adults. These institutions operate under the aegis of the National Council for Educational Awards, an organisation which has been at the forefront of educational developments in Ireland in recent years, especially in its efforts to widen the educational opportunities for adults.

Under the aegis of the Department of Agriculture, the Agricultural Advisory Service has provided an extensive range of courses for many years. Since 1979, the Council for the Development of Agriculture (ACOT) has been responsible for advisory services, and training and educational programmes in the agricultural sector. Seminars, short courses, part-time and full-time residential courses complement the wide range of services offered by ACOT. The Department of Health, through the Health Education Bureau, provides courses nationally on issues related to health. Regional Health Boards have, in recent years, appointed education officers to facilitate the provision of these courses throughout the country.

Voluntary organisations, both urban and rural, provide a myriad of courses for adults throughout Ireland. Sometimes they act as the sole providers of courses for their own members; at other times they provide courses in co-operation with other voluntary and statutory agencies.

Since their inception, many voluntary organisations in Ireland have been major promoters of adult education by encouraging their own members to participate in programmes and courses organised by themselves or by other bodies. Trades unions, churches and professional organisations also make significant contributions to developmental courses for adults. Industrial training courses for adults are provided by the Industrial Training Agency (AnCO) on a national basis while another agency, (CERT), provides education and training for staff in the hotel, catering and tourism industry. Remedial adult education, especially literary provision, is organised for the greater part by the National Adult Literacy Agency (NALA).

From the foregoing summary of provision, it is obvious that very few agencies have adult education as their central function and that even the major providers have adult education as a secondary, allied or subordinate function (Schroeder 1970). This situation will inevitably have major implications for the training of adult educators.

TRAINING OF ADULT EDUCATORS

Commenting on the various impediments to the development of adult education in Ireland, the Kenny Report (1984: 4, iii) states that 'there is a shortage of effective tutors of adults, particularly in rural areas. Very few have even elementary training and the official rate of remuneration is too low to provide an incentive.' Over a decade earlier, the Murphy Report (1973: 2.2.1.) had made the very same point much more forcefully:

> The fact must not be overlooked that many teachers, lecturers, education officers and teachers of voluntary organisations have been the real labourers in the field of adult education in Ireland; often receiving little or no training for their work with the adult learner, they have continued to serve their adult learners with a remarkable sense of commitment and skill.

To this day, the vast majority of tutors in Ireland are part-timers and a majority of these have no training in adult education. The part-time nature of their involvement raises difficulties regarding their participation in training courses. According to the Aontas directory (1985) training and formation programmes are divided into three main categories:

1 Initial training, formation and in-service training of full-time professional adult and community educators and development workers, organisers, youth leaders, tutors and organisers.
2 Training of part-time adult educators who receive a remuneration for their work.
3 Training of voluntary adult and community educators, leaders and workers.

However, according to the same source (Aontas 1985: 145):

> Training facilities for full-time adult and community
> educators are not plentiful in Ireland. Some few agencies
> provide full-time and part-time professional post-graduate
> diploma and higher degree courses in adult and community
> education. Some adult education agencies provide short
> training courses (seminars, workshops and summer schools)
> for the part-time adult educator, voluntary leader or
> community educator. Some agencies also provide initial and
> continuing inservice training for their staff who are involved
> in formal and non-formal adult education.

Only six institutions (four of which are universities) are listed in
the Aontas directory as providing full-time and/or part-time
courses for adult educators, while eight agencies (four of which
are universities) are mentioned as offering special courses or
workshops for this group.

Third-level institutions are generally regarded as the most
likely and the most competent agencies to provide education and
training for adult educators (Murphy 1973: 3.3.7., Kenny 1984:
Rec No. 27). Most Irish universities offer training courses for
adult educators, with Maynooth offering a Diploma in Adult
and Continuing Education and other universities offering part-
time certificates and shorter initial and in-service courses. Both
University College Cork and University College Galway
regularly offer courses ranging from one day, or weekend blocks,
to two terms for tutors of adults and for adult education
organisers. Some universities, e.g. University College Galway,
also include a module in adult education in both their general
teacher training and in their master's degree of education
programmes. Most universities offer courses for adult educators
in conjunction with the major providers of adult education, the
Vocational Education Committees, and with other statutory and
voluntary agencies. University College Dublin, with the help of
the Kellogg Foundation, has designed and offered training
programmes for adult educators and advisors in the agricultural
sector (Carter 1979). In Cork, the university, because of its
interest and work in the Third World, organises regular seminars
and workshops for those involved in developmental work.
University College Galway has recently launched a master's
degree programme in rural development for educators, trainers,
administrators and other workers in the field of rural community
development. However, in general, provision is rather piecemeal,
with the exception of that offered by Maynooth College, and if

the experience of University College Galway holds true with the other universities (and it probably does) then courses are usually provided for adult educators only when the request is first received from interested groups. Financial constraints, coupled with the status of adult education in general and also within the university system, militate against the regular provision of training programmes in adult education.

Other third-level institutions, such as the National Institute for Higher Education, the Dublin Institute of Technology, regional technical colleges and colleges of education, provide initial and in-service courses for their own tutors who may have little experience in adult education, and these are usually conducted by their own adult education officers, where they are in post. Distance learning programmes (NIHE Dublin) and in-service programmes for teachers (Thomond College of Education) have the potential for very exciting developments in the area of tutor training.

Statutory bodies, such as the Council for the Development of Agriculture (ACOT), the Industrial Training Agency (AnCO), Health Boards and the Health Education Bureau, as well as employer, trades union and church bodies all provide training opportunities for their own personnel, ranging from day and weekend seminars to more extended periods of in-service education and training.

Adult education organisers and personnel responsible for recruitment and training in voluntary organisations provide courses for tutors and trainers on a regular basis, either from their own resources or more often in collaboration with the universities or other institutes of education. Most of the Vocational Education Committees arrange short courses for their part-time tutors at regular intervals. University College Galway co-operates with adult education organisers of the Vocational Education Committees in providing several short courses annually for part-time tutors of adults in each of the western counties of Ireland. Similar joint programme are arranged in other parts of the country.

The National Adult Literacy Agency provides initial and regular in-service courses for its literacy tutors and organisers of literacy programmes. These training programmes are offered mostly at local or regional centres and the Agency also arranges national conferences on a regular basis.

Voluntary organisations, especially those with a rural orientation, such as Macra na Feirme, Muintir na Tire and the women's association, the Irish Countrywomen's Association, provide education and training courses for their own members, as well as providing these courses, either separately or sometimes in co-operation with other agencies, for members of other organisations.

Aontas is particularly active in promoting and arranging courses and seminars, mostly on a day or weekend basis, for personnel in adult education. Established in 1968 to promote and develop adult education in Ireland, it provides a facilitating structure for competence development among adult educators through regular publications, conferences, seminars, training sessions and its consultative, library and research facilities.

THE FUTURE

The above summary of trends in adult education demonstrates that the training of adult educators in Ireland still leaves a lot to be desired. In spite of many pronouncements and firm recommendations regarding the needs for more adequate training provision (Murphy 1973, Kenny 1984) little planned development has taken place. Most adult education is provided by agencies and tutors and organisers for whom adult education is a secondary, subordinate or allied function. Personnel from adult education who participate in training courses, more often than not, receive no credits for attendance — although, as has been shown, some third-level institutions do confer diplomas or certificates on course completion. Some teacher training courses now include at least a module on adult education and a few, like St Angela's College in Sligo, offer opportunities to teach adults in their official teaching practice programme.

Ireland is by no means unique in its apparent tardiness to confront the problem of how to advance the professional development of its adult educators. Factors which contribute to its low status (Purvis 1978) include structural location and the content, structure and process of adult education are almost certainly the major barriers to planned developmental opportunities for adult educators at national level. The 'invisibility' of adult education as a distinctive sector in Ireland, resulting in the lack of a common identity among the thousands of practitioners, the absence of a definite career structure and the primacy of the traditional areas of elementary, secondary and third-level education tend to confirm in people's minds the marginality of adult education.

There is little question concerning competence with regard to subject knowledge and expertise of the majority of part-time adult educators but there is a serious question about their level of knowledge of, and their expertise in, the process of adult education, i.e. how adults learn and how best a practitioner may contribute towards their development. Many people in the field, whether trained or untrained as teachers, have drifted into the work and have possibly had little opportunity to upgrade their knowledge and skills. Such a haphazard trend will do little to change the low value-estimate that so many people have of adult education.

World recession and inflation have not made things any easier for adult education in Ireland. Restricted budgets have meant that priorities in all the services have had to be identified. Education is no exception, and adult education from its low-status position is in direct competition for funds — not only from the general social services but from the other sectors of education. Adult education organisers face an increasingly difficult job of establishing programmes and retaining a cadre of competent tutors to service their programmes. Poor remuneration for tutors, in contrast to that offered by the more generously endowed educational agencies, compounds the problem.

Two suggestions made in the Rogers Report (1985) for Northern Ireland would, if implemented in the Republic, be of special help in this regard. The first is the provision of a staged programme of training of part-time tutors, i.e. at first level some 30 to 40 hours of training, at second level some 100 hours of training and at third level a full professional training programme (7.5-7.11). Such a staged programme would ensure the provision of facilitators, on an on-going basis, for initial and in-service courses for part-time tutors. The second suggestion refers to the thorny problem of financing such training courses. Rogers (8.3) suggests that if all the agencies of adult education were to allocate 5 per cent of their budgets to training and staff development, then training might be a more feasible objective for many agencies. In the Irish context, such implementation might entail some minimal curtailment of existing courses. However, the advantages to the system generally of providing such training courses would far outweigh any disadvantages.

Certainly an increasing body of knowledge and research in adult education exists. The availability of this knowledge and the facilitating structures to enable gifted amateurs among adult education tutors to share in it must be among the priorities for adult education in Ireland. Short pre-service courses, combined with regular opportunities for in-service training, planned at national level and available locally, would do much to enhance the status of adult education in Ireland and contribute to the professionalisation of its personnel.

BIBLIOGRAPHY

Aontas (1985) *Aontas: Directory of Adult and Community Education Agencies in Ireland*, Dublin: Aontas.

Boshier, R. (1985) 'Conceptual framework for analyzing the training of trainers and adult educators', *Convergence* vol XVIII, nos 3/4: 3-22

Carter, G.L. (1979) 'Designing inservice training for professional practitioner adult educators', *Aontas Review* vol 1, no 1: 25-30.

Clancy, P. (1982) *Participation in Higher Education*, Dublin: Higher Education Authority.

Hartman, M. (1983-4) 'Some surprises found in national survey of adult educators' *The Learning Connection* vol 5 no 1 Dec-Jan, LERN – Learning Resources Network.

IVEA (1986) *Partners in Education – the VEC Response*, Dublin: Irish Vocational Education Association.

Legge, D. (1985) 'Training of adult education workers in West Europe', *Convergence* vol XVIII, nos 3-4: 59-66.

NCEA (1978) *An Award Structure for Recurrent Education*, Dublin: NCEA.

— (1985) *Towards Facilitating Awards for Adult and Continuing Education: a discussion document*, Dublin: National Council for Educational Awards.

— (1985) *Extending Educational Opportunity through NCEA Awards by Distance Learning*, Dublin: NCEA.

O'Murchu, M.W. (1984) *Adult Education in Europe: Ireland*, Prague: European Centre for Leisure and Education, vols. 21-2.

Purvis, J. (1978) 'The low status of adult education – some sociological reflections', *Educational Research* vol 19, no 1: 13-24.

Report of a Committee appointed by the Minister of Education (1973) *Adult Education in Ireland* (Murphy Report), Dublin: Government Publications.

Report of a Committee of Inquiry appointed by the Secretary of State for Education and Science (1973) *Adult Education: A Plan for Development*, London: HMSO.

Report of a Working Party on the Training and Staff Development of Teachers in Continuing Education (1985) *Learning to Teach; Teaching to Learn* (Rogers report), Dublin: NICCE.

Report of Commission on Adult Education (1984) *Lifelong Learning* (Kenny Report), Dublin: Government Publications.

Schroeder, W.L. (1970) 'Adult education defined and described' in R.M. Smith, G.F. Aker and J.R. Kidd (eds) *Handbook of Adult Education*, New York: MacMillan.

UNESCO (1985) *Fourth International Conference on Adult Education: Final Report*, Paris: UNESCO.

5 Educators of adults in England and Wales

Derek Legge

THE PRESENT COMPLEXITY

The situation today in England and Wales is complicated by a large number of factors. 'Training' itself is regarded by some as an awkward and limiting word when thinking about educators of adults, although it is the word most commonly used. 'Preparation' might be a better word but to many this carries the suggestion of pre-service activity, whereas much of the training provision is for those already active in the field. For a long period, the training of adult educators was viewed with much disfavour, despite the evidence of its value which was provided as early as the eighteenth century by people such as Griffith Jones in Wales (Kelly 1970) and the advocacy of training in such reports as the '1919 Report' (Ministry of Reconstruction) and that of the British Institute of Adult Education and the Tutors' Association in 1928 (BIAE 1928). Thanks perhaps to the reports of more recent government committees of enquiry, such as the Russell Committee (DES 1973) and three from the Haycocks Committee (ACSTT 1975, 1978), there is now a greater acceptance of the idea of training. Even so, hostility and suspicion still linger, reflecting perhaps fears of over-rigidity and stereotyping rather than the alleged spontaneity and enthusiasm of the untrained worker, and partly old beliefs that only subject knowledge is necessary for teaching adults. Employing authorities tend to require subject qualifications, represented by a degree, a technical award or a craft certificate, but there is still no insistance on teaching qualifications in the adult sector. This contrasts with the requirement of 'qualified teacher status' for teachers of children. Most teachers of adults are, in fact, still without formal training, and the quality of their work is variable. Attitudes to training can vary from enthusiastic support, through lukewarm lip-service, to downright opposition, and the phrase 'an ounce of practice is worth a ton of theory' can still be heard.

The term 'adult educator' may also have many meanings.

Besides teachers there are organisers and administrators of education for adults, and though some are specialists, many have overlapping roles accepting duties as 'tutor-organisers', administrators who also teach, or advisors who may combine a multitude of tasks. In some subject areas, especially in sport, words like 'coach' or 'instructor' are used instead of 'teacher'. Sometimes these reflect older concepts of the work, especially the distinction between 'education' and 'training', and sometimes there are echoes of old, but still existing rivalries such as that between the providers of adult liberal education (which is general) and those concerned with more work-related subjects in 'further' or 'higher' education. If one accepts a broad view of the education of adults, it is also true that many of those active in the field do not recognise themselves as 'adult educators'. They may, therefore, not consider themselves eligible for any training provided or indeed think such training appropriate.

Any consideration of the provision of training has, therefore, to take into account a good number of diverse attitudes and tensions and to these have to be added a very diverse range of types of work. Besides a core of full-time teachers, organisers and administrators in colleges, adult education centres, universities and some voluntary organisations, there are a large number of part-time teachers, thousands of voluntary unpaid workers and, perhaps, an even greater number of those for whom the education of adults is at least a facet of their work. The latter would include librarians, social workers, industrial trainers, clergy, doctors, nurses and some prison and military personnel, those in community development work and those working in counselling and guidance services. Similarly people are active in many different settings: in colleges and centres in industry and government agencies such as the Training Agency (formerly the Manpower Services Commission); in correspondence work and other forms of distance education; in informal voluntary organisation activities; in 'outreach' work and even at home. It is difficult to get an accurate picture of the numbers involved — some would include the whole adult population as 'teachers' as well as 'learners' — but it seems probable that part-time employed teachers outnumber the full-time teachers by about two to one. There would also seem to be a considerable turnover of part-time staff, perhaps up to 30 per cent per annum; people do, in fact, enter and leave and, perhaps, re-enter the work, and the same is obviously true of the vast number of volunteer workers.

These factors have led to many questions and arguments which beset the provision of training for educators of adults in

England and Wales. Some ask what is the desirable ratio of full-time to part-time workers, and consequently on what type of training should limited resources be used. Should the provision be mainly pre-service, in-service or advanced? The present emphasis appears to be on in-service, but some argue vigorously for training before entry to the work. What is the relative value of a modular or a linear approach to training? How far should training be institution-dominated, or work-based, or perhaps organised on a very formal basis? What kind of content and method would be appropriate? Some stress the need for the absorption of academic knowledge whilst others believe that satisfactory training requires participative, experiential methods, leading to greater sensitivity and understanding and more 'desirable' attitudes. Should there be generic training for everyone or is there more need for special segregated courses? Should teachers, organisers and administrators, for example, all have the same training, or should they be trained separately at all times? Have teachers of different subjects special needs which must be met in different ways? Should, for example, teachers of engineering, philosophy, dance, craft work and literacy all be trained together or in distinct groups? Should subject competence be regarded as quite distinct from teaching competence? Disputes rage about objectives and the vital question, 'Why train?'.

THE PRESENT PROVISION

Against this background it is not surprising that the training of adult educators in England and Wales is full of diversity. Like the provision of education for adults as a whole, with its mixture of arrangements by local authorities, voluntary agencies, industry and commerce, universities, private legislation, etc. (Legge 1982), training often appears to be somewhat disorganised and not always consistent. There has been no real planning concerned with the whole range of training needs and instead of a neat, tidy programme there has been a proliferation of *ad hoc* and often limited schemes, each tending to become more separate. This is a situation which worries some adult educators and it has led to some plans for a more unified approach or, at least, the establishment of an acknowledged relationship between the schemes and their providers. Some support for this seems recently to have been forthcoming from the Department of Education and Science, which has called for attention to be given to rationalisation and a 'coherent system' of training, but plans are still at an early stage and face much critical opposition. A summary of the present position of training will perhaps best illustrate the problem.

THE LOCAL EDUCATION AUTHORITIES (LEAs)

Diversity in fact is still very apparent, even among local education authorities which are the major providers of training for educators of adults. There are over one hundred different local education authorities in England and Wales and some are very active in this field, but others are doing very little. After the Second World War, largely to cope with the needs of full-time staff in the institutions providing work-related education, four specialist LEA 'colleges of education (technical)' were established in Bolton, Huddersfield, London (Garnett College) and Wolverhampton. Most of these are now linked with polytechnics or other higher education institutions, and there have been some changes in the work that they carry out. Although they continue to provide one-year full-time courses in further education (16 to 25 year age group at below university level) they also provide two-year part-time courses and four-term sandwich courses which offer in-service training for those who already have substantial teaching commitments. In Wales, the University College of Cardiff and the University of Wales Institute of Science and Technology run a joint course which is one-year full-time and they also organise a shorter sandwich course. The courses in all five institutions lead to a certificate in education (FE) and to the recognition for qualified teacher status by the Department of Education and Science. With more than half the teachers in colleges of further education untrained in teaching competence, the emphasis is increasing on in-service training, and besides the more substantial courses already noted, some of the five institutions offer a range of short courses, conferences, study groups and workshops. Some, too, have moved to the provision of advanced courses leading to advanced diplomas or master's degree in technical education — again on a part-time and a full-time basis. In the Bolton College, for example, there is a Diploma of Advanced Study in Technical Education. Some of the polytechnics have also established departments of education offering professional teacher training, and a few colleges of art now provide independent training for teachers of art.

The first report of the Haycocks Committee of the Advisory Committee on the Supply and Training of Teachers (1975) — referred to as ACSTT 1 1975 — made recommendations concerning the training needs of full-time teachers particularly in the work-related sector, and these have guided the provision made, particularly in the five specialist institutions referred to above. The second 'Haycocks Report' (ACSTT 2 1978) looked at the needs of part-time teachers of adults across the whole spectrum of subject interests and took into account the needs of those with even the minimum teaching commitments of only two hours per week. Published in 1978, this report was never endorsed by the Department of Education and Science but many LEAs have acted upon it and have either provided new schemes of training for part-time teachers of adults or else they have modified their existing ones. Some had, in fact, already experimented with training part-time teachers for many years, especially in Yorkshire, the East Midlands and the North West. Action in this provision by the LEAs is now usually under the auspices of the Regional Advisory Councils (RACs), of which there are nine in England. Wales has a similar body called the Wales Joint Education Committee (WJEC) and this has similar functions. Each of these, although dominated by the LEAs, brings together representatives of all relevant interests including, for example, those of commerce, industry and the universities. Both the type of representation and the overall function, however, vary according to the characteristics of the region that they serve. Established in the post-war era, their original concern was to develop the regional planning of work-related courses, but many have now widened their role to encompass all aspects of post-16 sector non-university education (until 1989 when polytechnic higher education also moved away from LEA control). As their finances come mainly from the LEAs, their main concern has tended to be LEA work. But, in terms of training, their interests have broadened from oversight of schemes for full-time teachers to a growing concern for the provision of part-time teacher training. Over half of the RACs now sponsor schemes which are based on the recommendations of the second Haycocks Report, and the most developed of these offer a three-stage modular course:

1   A brief consideration of basic teaching skills — about 36 to 40 hours in length.
2   This offers a substantial series of modules designed to improve the skills and understanding of teachers and to extend their sensitivity to the learning needs of students — about 100 hours in length.
3   This comprises a longer series of modules, perhaps requiring 300 hours or more in length and includes some in-depth

studies and attention to areas of special interest.

Attendance may be spread over a fairly long period of time but satisfactory completion of all three stages leads to the award of Certificate of Education (FE), as awarded to full-time teachers. It is assumed that the part-time teachers will already have recognised competence in the subject that they teach, so that the whole scheme concentrates on teaching competence with supervised teaching practice taking place in all three stages, although not a great deal in the first one.

In areas where a fully developed scheme has been offered many part-timers have taken Stage 1; an unexpectedly high number have also moved on to Stage 2 but a much smaller number have begun to take Stage 3. It should be noted that less than 40 per cent of the part-time teachers of adults are school teachers who also work with children. The courses are run by LEAs in their own colleges and centres and are staffed by those working full-time in the field, often in an advisory capacity. The RACs exercise supervision through a special committee or board of studies composed of LEA representatives who are often drawn from the training staff. Each course usually has to submit its curriculum for the approval of this committee and in some areas the committee appoints moderators, or mentors or assessors (again drawn from the full-time staff), whose function is to ensure that the quality of provision is maintained. Some of these regions are now beginning to include representation from the voluntary agencies on their committees.

Special provision for basic education teachers has also developed throughout the country with LEAs receiving financial support as well as advice from the Adult Literacy and Basic Skills Unit (ALBSU) which was established by the Department of Education and Science and the Welsh Office, and which operates as a agency of the National Institute of Adult Continuing Education (NIACE). Training courses are again organised, usually under the auspices of the RACs, which also supervise the distribution of ALBSU resources. A few individual LEAs have developed their own schemes of training in this sector and have made arrangements for special, usually segregated, training for those who teach disadvantaged adults. An example of such a special course is that held at the Central London Institute (City Literary Institute) for teachers of lip reading for adults. The Inner London Education Authority (abolished under recent government legislation) was particularly active in developing its own training schemes.

CITY AND GUILDS OF LONDON INSTITUTE (CGLI)

In many LEA institutions, usually colleges of further or higher education, there are courses held in the daytime or evening which lead to the award of the Further and Adult Education Teachers' Certificate — Course no 7307, which is offered by the City and Guilds of London Institute for both full-time and part-time teachers who are qualified in their subject but lacking teaching qualifications. City and Guilds is an independent body, founded in 1878 by the livery companies of London, to help the development of technical education. Course 7307 requires a part-time attendance of about 150 hours and a minimum of 30 hours' teaching practice. It provides a study of the principles and methods of teaching adults with a broad syllabus, leaving the training institution, e.g. the local college, a good deal of responsibility for the exact content, organisation and methods. City and Guilds, however, has established a system of area assessors to co-ordinate the standards of achievement.

In recent years, after its initial concern with technical education, City and Guilds has paid more attention to the needs of teachers working in the non-work related sector. Some pioneer experiments have been organised and Course 730 has been modified into Stages 1 and 2, more in line with the recommendations of the second Haycocks Report. For those with a Further Education Teacher's Certificate there is the chance of moving to a Further Education Advanced Certificate, which requires some 200 hours of attendance and includes a study of the aims and organisation of education for adults. Course 730 attracts candidates from the health services, industrial training establishments, HM Forces, and from teachers in LEA colleges and centres. Each year there are about 6,000 candidates.

THE ROYAL SOCIETY OF ARTS (RSA)

Another independent institution which offers examinations and certificates to those who follow courses in most colleges of further education and similar institutions is the Royal Society of Arts, originally founded in 1754. Besides a wide range of certificates, especially in commerce and business studies, the RSA offers diplomas and certificates for teachers in certain subject areas. These include:

- Teaching of English as a foreign language to adults.
- Teaching of English as a second language in further, adult

and community education.
* Teaching of literacy skills to adults.
* Teaching of foreign languages to adults.
* Teaching of community languages.
* Teaching of communication skills.
* Teacher's diploma in shorthand, typewriting and office procedure.
* Teacher's diploma in computer studies.
* Teacher's diploma in the use of computers in education.

These courses, which stress the subject areas, are usually located in the LEA colleges, which also serve as examination centres, and they are supervised by the RSA Council, detailed work being carried out by advisory committees and the day-to-day control delegated to an examination board. Several thousand teachers take these courses each year.

COLLEGE OF PRECEPTORS

A third independent body, founded in 1846, serves as an international professional membership body for teachers and other educators, and this also provides in-service courses and qualifications for experienced practitioners. These include the Associate Diploma (Associate of the College of Preceptors — ACP), the Licentiate Diploma (LCP) and the Fellowship Diploma (FCP). within the ACP there is a special Further Education Staff Training Course from which candidates may proceed by part-time day or evening courses to the LCP. Thus far this route has been taken mainly by full-time staff, but a few part-timers have been allowed to take it provided that they will have completed at least 700 hours teaching experienced by the end of the course. These courses are also held in further education colleges and the trainers are usually experienced and senior members of the college staff. If the college is suitably equipped, e.g. has an adequate library and experienced staff, it can propose an internal scheme of training for its new staff and this can lead to the award of an ACP after external validation.

INDEPENDENT VOLUNTARY ORGANISATIONS

Much education of adults, both formal and non-formal, is provided by thousands of voluntary associations, some are large and have a national orientation, e.g. the Workers' Educational

Association, Women's Institute and the Townswomen's Guild, while others are small and have a local orientation, such as a village history club or a local craft society. Some of the larger organisations have paid full-time staff, while others depend entirely on unpaid voluntary work carried out by annually elected officers and committees. The vast majority receive no grants from government sources and rely on membership fees or money-raising efforts. Some have had a long history but others are short-lived and depend in part on meeting changing needs and interests and also upon available resources and personnel.

Their durability also depends upon the quality of the voluntary or the paid workers. Two enquiries commissioned in 1980 and 1983 by the former Advisory Council for Adult and Continuing Education (ACACE 1983) revealed that over 200 voluntary organisations had developed a keen interest in the training of their officers and staff, and that some had detailed and substantial schemes of their own for this purpose; the latter included organisations like: the British Red Cross Society, St John Ambulance Association, the National Federation of Women's Institutes, the National Union of Townswomen's Guilds, the Pre-School Playgroups Association, the Keep-Fit Association, the Young Men's Christian Association, National Association of Citizen's Advice Bureaux and some dance societies such as the Medau Society and the Laban Guild. Some of these schemes required as much as 270 hours of attendance and were considered to be equivalent to the CGLI 7307 course or Stages 1 and 2 of the RAC schemes. While some give considerable emphasis to subject competence as the key to good quality teaching, e.g. the competitive sports, others use LEA courses to provide the element of general teaching competence, while retaining firm control over the subject. Some of these schemes are critical of the RAC schemes for being too 'institution slanted' and for showing little appreciation of informal and non-formal learning outside colleges and centres. Even so, the Central Council for Physical Recreation, which brings together many voluntary organisations, has been attempting to adapt the CGLI 7307 course to meet the requirements of teachers of movement and dance, and there have also been experiments in joint training between RACs and organisations such as the Keep-Fit Association and the Pre-School Playgroups Association. One of the problems is that there is a good deal of ignorance about the roles and structures of the various bodies concerned with training and this results in misconceptions which create barriers between the various bodies.

THE UNIVERSITIES

A few universities have been interested for over half a century in the education and training of professional educators of adults; more recently fifteen universities were shown to be involved (Standing Conference on University Teaching and Research in the Education of Adults 1983). Most of the contribution to training is at a post-graduate level leading to advanced diplomas in adult education, or community education or continuing education, or to master's degrees by both research or taught programmes (in England and Wales there are two distinct types of master's degree — the one by teaching is usually one-year full-time or two-years part-time and involves the completion of course work plus a small research dissertation, whilst the research mater's requires candidates to complete a research thesis and may involve a little course work). In addition, nine universities offer doctoral research supervision in adult education. In a rather smaller number, the education of adults forms part of a post-graduate certificate in education course while a few offer specific courses in teaching adults: the University of Nottingham offers a Certificate in Adult Teaching and the University of Surrey a Post-Graduate Certificate in the Education of Adults.

With few exceptions, most of the students in university courses are educators of adults who are in their mid-career. As it has become increasingly difficult for senior, experienced adult educators to obtain release from their work, most now study on a part-time basis although it might be argued that a period of full-time study away from their jobs is likely to be of the greatest benefit. Some people believe that the best contribution that universities can make to training is good library facilities, opportunity for reflection, experiment and study, and arrangements for contact with many types of educational activity as well as with other educators of adults. In the universities, however, there are differences of viewpoint, some believing that there should be greater stress on academic knowledge and a controlled curriculum with less emphasis on experiential learning. This is reflected in the staffing of the responsible university departments, some appointing mainly academic specialists while others insist on substantial practical experience in the education of adults. Several hundred people have now taken university courses and many of these now tend to supervise and conduct Haycocks-type courses in their regions. A few universities, such as Nottingham, have also developed seminars for educators of adults in their region, and also conduct summer schools of a week's duration. In Loughborough University of Technology, the

Centre for Extension Studies has developed a special training programme in the management of adult education. This is intended for principals and vice-principals working mainly in centres of non-work related adult education, or even in general studies departments of colleges of further and higher education. This takes the form of linked residential seminars, each of one week's duration.

THE OPEN UNIVERSITY

Problems of travel and attendance surround many forms of training for educators of adults and at times these act as a severe deterrent. The Open University, being aware of this, has made a special contribution by developing distance-learning courses in this area, including:

* A series of video-led resource packs which deal with the needs of adult learners and the processes of learning and teaching — suitable for initial training.
* Sets of print, audio and visual material designed to give practising teachers opportunities for further professional development.
* A range of undergraduate courses, such as 'Education for Adults' and 'Management in Post-Compulsory Education' — both of which can be taken by associate students who are not reading for a degree.
* Some specialist material in areas like telephone teaching and counselling.

In producing this material there has been close contact with adult educators and practising trainers in order to make it directly relevant to the needs of those in the field. Some of it is now being used widely.

PROBLEMS AND FUTURE NEEDS

To this multitude of providers and the diversity of training schemes in England and Wales can be added instructor training carried out by some commercial institutions and industry, including a new City and Guilds of London Institute course in training. There is also an arrangement whereby some special programmes for teachers of adults are broadcast by the British Broadcasting Corporation, including a series on 'Teaching

69

Adults'. There is a good deal of informal training in staff meetings, visits by advisers to classes, informal meetings of adult educators and the reading of professional journals. Several self-instructional teacher handbooks or manuals of advice have been issued in recent years by the providing agencies and there have been an increasing number of books and pamphlets on teaching and learning. The National Institute of Adult Continuing Education has contributed a good deal by its publications, especially by its journals and series on 'Teaching Adults' and also by its conferences and other meetings. Other professional bodies, such as the National Association of Teachers in Further and Higher Education (NATFHE) and the Association of Recurrent Education (ARE) have also provided opportunities for the development of greater competence.

Some may think that this is enough, but a number of problems stand out. There is an obvious need to bring about some cohesion to this varied provision and much more attention needs to be paid to the training of the trainers of those who work in adult education. It has been argued that the quality of the provision depends upon the competence of those trainers who conduct the training schemes and that they must also receive training and support. At present some RACs are offering such training, although it is rather *ad hoc* and of short duration, maybe a day or so a year. Some voluntary associations in the ACACE enquiries (ACACE 1983 and Legge *et al.* 1985) suggested that although they were endeavouring to make such provision themselves, they regarded its inadequacy as a major weakness largely because they lacked the necessary resources. As indicated above, some university departments offer an overall training but the problem remains as to how to get sufficient competent people. There have been some moves towards joint co-operative training of trainers from both the LEAs and the voluntary organisations, but this has thus far been on a very small scale.

Similarly, training for management in adult education institutions needs much development. The existing training of educators has tended to concentrate on the needs of teachers with the result that the training of all policy makers and planners is still very limited. The provision in Loughborough University of Technology, noted above, makes a good contribution and to this can be added the City and Guilds advanced certificate courses, the College of Preceptors courses and some of the provision from the polytechnics and larger colleges. However, this provision touches only a minority. Similarly, only a relatively small number of organisers and administrators have taken part in special provision made by the Further Education Staff College (FESC) at Coombe Lodge, which was established in 1962. At this college there have been residential study conferences, in which principals, vice-principals and heads of departments in the LEA colleges have come together to discuss problems of management, sometimes with key people from industry. The third Haycocks report (ACSTT 3 1978) drew attention to the great variety of levels in which management skills are required and to the vital need to make these more effective in the adult education sector, but so far developments have been very limited. In the voluntary organisations, training opportunities in management are even more restricted. Handbooks and short courses are provided by the Women's Institute and the Townswomen's Guild to give guidance to their members undertaking office, and some WEA branch officers discuss organisational problems over half-day or full-day meetings, but more often the voluntary worker struggles with a managerial role without preparation or help.

Thus far there has also been only a very restricted amount of training for counsellors and advisors in the education of adults, although the establishment of a National Association of Educational Guidance Services (NAEGS) in 1982 seems likely to help improve this situation. One of its aims is to 'facilitate the training of all those involved in providing the services' and there have been pilot training schemes in East Anglia and Yorkshire and Humberside. The 1986 report of the Unit for the Development of Adult Continuing Education (UDACE) on educational guidance proposes that every guidance network should have a policy of staff development and that full training opportunities should be made available, which should include general induction courses, assistance with special management problems and training in both generic and specialist skills.

The provision of training for all types of education for adults in England and Wales is, of course, surrounded by problems of finance and the resulting general uncertainty about resources. Too much still rests on the efforts and good will of a relatively small number of people working with inadequate support. Many would argue, too, that besides the urgent need for more resources a considerable change in attitude is required. There is still a belief that training can be a one-off matter whereas it is clear that there should be support for recurrent training so that all those providing education for adults will be helped throughout their working lives to be more effective in the work that they are doing. Perhaps training in many ways depends upon self-help, and the true professional is the one who continues to be self-critical and to use all the possible methods of improving competence. In methods and approach, the present emphasis upon training of adult educators seems to focus on 'learning by doing' with a great deal of use of project method, role play, case studies, field visits, micro-teaching, micro-planning and groupwork. Possibly this has weakened some of the opposition of those who feared a closed exclusive caste with rigid controls, but it has also raised critical opposition. Disagreements about methods and content and about the whole question of professionalisation, however, are probably healthy and likely to benefit the development of training. It seems to be more frequently acknowledged that even the most inspired missionary would benefit from some practical training, and that there is a growing feeling that participants in the education of adults have the right to expect the best possible support for their efforts to learn. In these terms training becomes a necessity.

BIBLIOGRAPHY

Advisory Council for Adult and Continuing Education (1983) *Teachers of Adults: Voluntary Specialist Training and Evaluating Training Courses*, Leicester: NIACE.

Advisory Committee on the Supply and Training of Teachers (1975) *The Training of Teachers for Further Education*, London: Department of Education and Science.

ACSTT (2) (1978) *The Training of Adult Education and Part-Time Further Education Teachers*, London: DES.

ACSTT (3) (1980) *Training Teachers for Education Management in Further and Adult Education*, London: DES.

British Institute of Adult Education and Tutors' Association (1928) *The Tutor in Adult Education: an Enquiry into the Problems of Supply and Training*, Carnegie Trust.

Charnley, A., Osborn, M. and Withnal, A. (1982) *Training the Educators of Adults: Review of Existing Research in Adult and Continuing Education*, Leicester: NIACE.

DES (1973) *Adult Education: A Plan for Development* (Russell Report), London: DES.

Elsdon, K. (1975) *Training for Adult Education*, Nottingham: University of Nottingham, Dept of Adult Education.

Elsdon, K. (1984) *The Training of Trainers*, Nottingham: Huntingdon Press in association with University of Nottingham; Dept of Adult Education.

Graham, T.B., Daines, J., Sullivan, T., Harris, P. and Benim, F.E. (1982) *The Training of Part-Time Teachers of Adults*, University of Nottingham, Department of Adult Education.

Jarvis, P. (1983) *Adult Education: Theory and Practice*, London: Croom Helm.

Kelly, T. (1950) *Griffith Jones Landowror, Pioneer in Adult Education*,

Liverpool: University of Wales.

Legge, D. (1982) *The Education of Adults in Britain*, Milton Keynes: Open University Press.

Legge, D., Chadwick, A. and Gilbert, H. (1985) *Training Opportunities for Teachers of Adults*, Leicester: NIACE.

Ministry of Reconstruction (1919) *Adult Education Committee Final Report*, London: HMSO.

Standing Conference on University Teaching and Research in the Education of Adults (1983) *Guide to University Courses for Adult Educators in the United Kingdom and Eire*.

Unit for Development of Adult Continuing Education (1986) *The Challenge of Change: Developing Educational Guidance for Adults*, Leicester: NIACE.

Part III

Franco-Mediterranean countries

6   The training of adult educators in France

Pierre Freynet

It is impossible to discuss the training of adult educators in France without first attempting to define adult education. The term does not necessarily have the same meaning in different countries. From the outset, it must be recognised that the term is infrequently employed in France, terms like 'continuing training', 'permanent education', 'popular education', etc. all have great currency.

It would be confusing, therefore, if the term were not made clear from the start. At first sight, the expression appears sufficiently clear and straightforward. Nevertheless, on closer examination, the use of the terms 'adult' and 'education' in France are far from straightforward. While there is no need to engage in a purely academic debate, it is necessary to clarify the terms, since their institutional use tends to obscure their meaning.

WHAT IS MEANT BY 'ADULT'?

It is not necessary to question the use of the term 'adult' nor to enter into the criticisms of the term, but Lapassade (1963) calls into question the idea of completion which it implies rather than the idea of fulfilment throughout the whole of life. More concretely, it is necessary to consider the fact that one can actually see in France that the division between the recipients of education is not actually between children and adults. In effect, what has been happening for several years now has been the emergence of a new category of those who might be described as 'youth', that is those who have completed their statutory schooling (i.e. 16 years of age) but have not yet entered work or further study. For such groups as these, according to Schwartz (1981), major categories have been devised that relate to courses for social and professional entry and those which lead to additional qualifications. Adopting UNESCO definitions, we have to consider those who are between 16 and 21, or even 25, years of age as adults, but in France the term adolescent is preferred — even more than the term 'youth'.

In our opinion, even though such strategies have been financed by the Ministry of Professional Training, it all reduces the quality of provision in the school system. However one views it, it is an admission of failure if a school system cannot guarantee to those who pass through it either adequate training or entry into an occupation. It is this kind of professional transition that the strategies for young people have tried to achieve. It is in our opinion a 'second-chance schooling', rather than an adult strategy.

These youth training courses have, however, taken place in an institutional setting different from that of compulsory schooling: they have not been financed nor organised by the Ministry of Education but by that of Professional Training; they have not been staffed by teachers, but rather by trainers especially recruited either from continuing training programmes of the National Education organisation (GRETA) or else from private training organisations or from popular education associations.

At the same time as the emergence of these youth strategies, there has also developed an increasing number of training and other activities directed towards those referred to not so much as the 'elderly' but as being of the 'third age'.

As in the case of the young, where it has been important to facilitate the transition between school and work, so it is necessary with the 'third age' to help bring about the transition from an active to a less active life. This is sometimes achieved at the workplace in the form of pre-retirement courses. It should be added that this new category of 'third age' includes the pre-retirement stage of between 55 and 60 years of age.

These two categories, the youth and the elderly, have assumed a numerical significance: the first, because they constitute a large proportion of the total unemployed; the second, because for demographic and economic reasons their relative importance in the population of France is growing. In fact, apart from this distinction between the young and the elderly, the criterion of age would appear to be of little account. Much more important is the situation with regard to the working life which lies ahead of the young and behind the elderly.

Similarly for other participants of adult education, the work situation is very important. Thus it is necessary to distinguish between:

The unemployed.

- Wage earners during their normal hours of work.
- Wage earners outside their normal hours of work.

In greatly simplifying the situation in France, which is extremely complex, and in attempting to give the term 'adult' a general significance which corresponds to that given it in other countries and to that ascribed to it by UNESCO, it is possible to derive the following typology of client groups for adult education in France:

- Youth, seeking employment and under 25 years of age.
- The unemployed.
- Wage earners during their normal hours of work.
- Wage earners outside their normal hours of work.
- The 'third age'.

WHAT IS MEANT BY 'EDUCATION'?

Here again it is unnecessary to enter into a debate about the fundamental principles of education. But in so far as the term 'adult education' is used in France, it is important to understand to what it actually refers. In fact, there is a long tradition but it has tended to be referred to as 'popular education'. This was essentially the work of voluntary organisations and activists. Such associations were, and still are very numerous and amounted to a very important movement. In those cases where their activities were recognised by the state and institutionalised, the movement has been transformed into what is usually called today 'socio-cultural *animation*', with its own premises (Centres of Youth and Culture, Centres for Everyone, Neighbourhood Centres, etc.) with activities mainly orientated towards leisure (dance, theatre, yoga, painting, macramé, etc.). Its clientele, moreover, is not limited to adults but include large numbers of young people, both those at school and those who have left school. In fact, it is as much about 'non-formal' as 'adult' education. The history of adult education in France came to a turning point with the law on 16 July 1971 which concerned training. This law, in particular, requires employing firms, with at least ten employees, to set aside 0.8 per cent of their wages bill (soon to be raised to 1 per cent) for continuing training. Firms are at liberty to choose the form of training provision, or even to provide it themselves.

Following popular education movements, a market has been established. However, the law of 1971 also meant that the state began to play a larger role and, indeed, the state provides a large proportion of the overall financial investment in continuing training. However, there has also been some decentralisation of professional training, so that the twenty-one regions of France also constitute very important partners.

Looked at overall, an increasing number of activities are organised especially for the 'third-age' group. Many universities, for example, have established 'universities of the third age', whilst many associations are also represented in this work with the elderly. Third-age activities comprise numerous conferences, modern language courses and socio-cultural activities, such as painting, macramé, bridge, basket-weaving, etc.

In our opinion, a view of adult education in France needs to include:

- Courses of social and professional preparation and qualification.
- Courses for young adults (16 to 25 years of age).
- Socio-cultural *animation*, for adults.
- Continuing training in the workplace
  (a) as part of a firm's training programme (employer's initiative);
  (b) in the form of individual study leave (employee's initiative).
- Continuing training for employees outside their normal working hours, usually in the evenings (social advancement), and financed by the regions.
- Specific training for the unemployed; generally financed by the state.
- Third-age training and activities.

This scheme, although simplified, could still appear somewhat complex, but is necessary in order to understand the general situation in France.

WHAT ORGANISATIONS PROVIDE ADULT EDUCATION IN FRANCE?

Although initial training is centralised, adult education is not. There exists no national structure for adult education, but rather very diverse bodies, dependent upon different ministries and forms of funding. In fact, despite public financing, there is still a market in continuing training, functioning along a needs-meeting line.

It is not possible to describe all the bodies concerned with adult training, so that the most that can be done is to provide some broad outlines of the system:

* Socio-cultural *animation* is usually provided by the associations for popular education, established at a national level, and whose origins go back to the liberation of 1945, or to the Popular Front of 1936, or even in some cases to the end of the nineteenth century — with the establishment of state education. It is possible to mention, among others, the French Education League, the French Federation of Centres of Youth and Culture, People and Culture, the Léo Lagrange Federation, etc. All of these organisations depend upon the Ministry for Leisure, Youth and Sport, and are financed partly by the ministry and partly by the municipalities.

* The training of young people between the ages of 16 and 25 years, financed by the Ministry for Professional Training, is provided to a large extent by the same associations, and to some extent by the continuing training services of National Education, or GRETA (about 50 per cent), and on a smaller scale by other private bodies.

* Continuing training in industry is financed by the employers and is provided by very diverse organisations
  (a) the firms themselves, especially the larger ones
  (b) organisations concerned with training (ASFO)
  (c) chambers of commerce and industry
  (d) insurance funds (mutual benefit societies)
  (e) continuing training services of National Education, or GRETA
  (f) private, profit-making training organisations.

* Continuing training for workers outside their normal working hours, generally called social advancement and financed by the regions, which is most often provided by the institutions of National Education, the universities and GRETA. These generally rely for their training courses upon teachers in secondary and high schools.

* Specific training for the unemployed, which is often automatically financed by the state, may be provided by a range of organisations (National Education, associations, chambers of commerce and industry, private bodies, etc.)

* Third-age training and activities are generally run by the universities or by voluntary associations.

WHO ARE THE ADULT EDUCATORS IN FRANCE?

Since adult education can refer to such a diverse range of activities, there is little reference in this country to adult educators — the term 'educator' being reserved mainly for more specialist forms of education. In fact, a number of different terms are used, depending upon the situation:

- Youth trainers, for those who work with the 16 to 25 year age group.
- *Animateurs*, for those who work in socio-cultural *animation* and popular education.
- Adult trainers, for courses of the continuing type, which are financed either by firms, local communities or the state.

THE STATUS OF ADULT EDUCATORS

Here also there obviously exists a very diverse situation. The status of the trainer is constantly raised as an issue in discussions of socio-cultural *animation* and training.

As far as *animateurs* are concerned, their activities vary widely: resource managers, co-ordinators of activities, organisers of activities, etc., all of which makes it very difficult to establish a distinct status for the profession. They are increasingly working at the boundaries of social problems and culture, rather as if, writes Besnard (1981), '*animation*, at the congruence of the social and the cultural, functioned as a cultural response, sometimes educational, to social problems and issues'. Indeed, *animateurs* are considered by the Ministry of Social Affairs as though they were social workers. However, despite such problems of identity, their profession (there were 25,000 *animateurs* in France in 1982) is recognised as one which meets a continuing and growing need.

One cannot say the same for youth trainers. In effect, the various strategies aimed at young people leaving school without qualifications or certificates were originally presented as only a temporary measure. Funding was, therefore, available on a year-to-year basis. Trainers on these courses are recruited for the duration of the course only and one of the main demands of these trainers is for a more clearly defined status.

The case of the trainers on courses organised within industry is equally variable. Many of them have adopted the status of independent workers, and are therefore regarded as members of the professional classes. Others are employed by various private agencies for continuing training. It is impossible to identify clearly the national status of adult trainers.

Courses for 'social advancement' are generally conducted in the evenings and are taught by school teachers who are paid an additional salary for this work.

Third-age courses and activities are usually run by volunteers and, in certain organisations, by *animateurs*.

It is obvious that for the sake of clarity, we have tried to simplify this account of the diverse forms of status of the trainers. In practice, the situation is much more complicated, not least because the different activities are often conducted within the same institution and even by the same person, who can be regarded at the same time as an *animateur*, youth trainer, organiser, etc.

WHAT QUALIFICATIONS EXIST FOR ADULT EDUCATORS?

This issue is obviously closely related to the last one. As compared with teachers in initial education, who enjoy a systematic career structure clearly demarcated by a range of tests, examinations, diplomas, grades, etc., the various types of adult educators badly lack such a structure in their own field, so that we need to examine the different categories separately.

The *animateurs*, perhaps because of the early origins of their movement, are certainly the best placed in respect of diplomas. Their work comes under three ministries:

1 National Education — this has University Diplomas in Technology (*baccalauréat* level plus two years) — in the socio-cultural animation option of social work, several degrees and master's degrees, especially those in the social work option of applied social science, which are open to all social workers.
2 The Ministry of Social Affairs — with its Higher Diploma in Social Work (DSTS).
3 The Ministry of Leisure which, in conjunction with the Ministry of Social Affairs, offers a Diploma in Administration, with a specialisation in *animation* (DEFA).

The youth trainers are less well served as no national qualification exists especially for them. However, a number of short courses (140 hours) have been provided for them and, in some instances, there are opportunities to study for a longer period (140 more hours) leading to a university diploma.

As for the adult trainers, they face a rather peculiar situation since there are very few national qualifications, e.g. first or master's degrees, in the training of adults but, on the other hand, there are many university qualifications and qualifications from other institutions.

In fact, to the extent that there exists a market in continuing training, the training of trainers is also organised along market lines and includes further training courses of various lengths and levels. Many industrial trainers, moreover, have not received any training in their own fields.

WHAT TRAINING EXISTS FOR ADULT EDUCATORS?

We have spent some time presenting the general approach to adult education in France before coming to the crux of this chapter, the training of adult educators. Nevertheless, this long introduction is necessary since the training of educators is itself conditioned by the institutional context in which it is conducted. In effect, while one cannot speak in France of the training of adult educators, one can speak of the training of *animateurs* or the training of 'trainers'. Furthermore, it is useful to distinguish between:

- The initial training of adult educators.
- The continuing training and knowledge updating of adult educators by way of short courses.
- Courses leading to higher qualifications for adult educators.

The initial training of adult educators

Oddly enough, this is very limited. Whilst teachers in initial training have a very structured training, adult educators rarely obtain suitable preparation for their work. All too often cases could be cited, such as the DUT socio-cultural *animation* option in social work (intensive training of 1,920 hours over two years, usually comprising a theoretical element, study of the institutional context and familiarisation with *animation* techniques). The majority of adult educators, whether they are volunteers or professionals, begin their work before undergoing any training in the field, as though it were tacitly assumed that people entering upon the work of continuing training did not need to have received it themselves. It is, therefore, in this area that most training is needed.

Short training courses for adult educators

The *animateur* or trainer who wishes to undergo further training in areas such as human relations, administration, computing, alternative methods, etc. will be embarrassed for choice: numerous organisations (both public and private) offer courses of varying duration — weekends, information days, courses of several weeks — or, indeed, months. Under this heading of short courses the 140-hour training period for youth trainers might also be included.

Higher-level qualifications for adult educators

These are much more numerous than those for initial training, but they exist in a very uncoordinated market provision. An exhaustive description of these cannot be given here but a general picture is offered. In summary form:

- Degree-level courses for *animateurs*: The best known of these is the Diploma in Administration, with specialisation in *animation* (DEFA). This course is intended for those who already have some professional experience and lasts for at least three years. It consists of:
  (a) a general course of five units, plus a practical placement. These units cover management, administration and organisation; pedagogy and human relations; *animation* techniques; the social context of *animation*; advanced *animation* techniques, or further work in one of the other topics.
  (b) a full-time place in *animation* for nine months, during which time the candidate must undertake a minimum of 240 hours of practical training.
  (c) a final evaluation.
- *Animateurs* who are considered social workers may prepare themselves for the Higher Diploma in Social Work (DSTS). In order to gain this diploma as an *animateur* they need to have had five years of professional experience in social work and 500 hours of preparatory training. The DSTS consists of three options: professional, training and social work research.
- *Animateurs* may also prepare themselves for the degree of Master in Applied Social Science (social work option) which is also restricted to social work graduates who have had five years' work experience.

Several universities (Paris XII, Strasbourg II, St Etienne, Toulouse, La Mirail, Limoges, Angers and Amiens) have together formed a network (RIFF) to provide preparation for both the first and the master's degree in applied social science, based upon research. These degrees are sometimes organised jointly with the DSTS.

The training of trainers in the universities

It is often believed that in France the universities have played a prominent role in the training of trainers. Now, despite much discussion and numerous debates and articles, it is clear that whilst their role has not been negligible it has been rather limited. Foudriat (1986) has suggested that the contribution made by the universities to the training of trainers is characterised by its diversity in several respects:

- in respect of its clientele;
- in respect of its duration — from 200 hours to two years;
- in respect of university standards, which range from *baccalauréat* plus one year to *baccalauréat* plus five years (DESS);
- in respect of the aims of training, which may be formulated along either professional or discipline lines;
- in respect of the type of validation, national or university certification.

Foudriat's research reveals that twenty-four universities organised a total of thirty-two training courses (or about one-third of the total). It showed, moreover, that the training of trainers represented only a very small proportion of all the continuing training work of the universities. It should also be remembered that certain universities offer university diplomas (DUFA) which validate the training of youth trainers.

Other training qualifications

The universities are by no means the only source of training for trainers seeking qualifications. A number of major private, public and voluntary organisations offer training either for their own or other trainers. In particular, many large training bodies, such as AFPA (Association pour la Formation Professionelle des Adultes) or National Education (with CAFOC) have their own systems of trainer training. Unfortunately there exists no exhaustive list of all the training courses for trainers. However, a certain number of organisations are now well known in the field, although others are less so. Indeed, it has to be borne in mind that many of these courses are quite well established whilst some of the university ones are of comparatively recent origin.

WHAT KIND OF PROGRAMMES ARE AVAILABLE IN THE TRAINING OF TRAINERS?

We have reviewed the programmes for the training of the *animateurs*, but we have not yet examined those for the trainers themselves. These, it will be seen, are also very diverse, according to the institution, the level, the duration, the qualification, etc. It may help to clarify matters if two client groups are initially identified:

- the trainers themselves,
- those responsible for the training.

In general, it is perhaps possible to argue that the training provided by the private organisations is more professionally orientated than that provided by the universities. In 1974 Ballier and Lambert, in a study of private organisations' training courses, devised a number of different categories which might be compared to those of Foudriat's (1986) study of universities' provision of trainer training mentioned above. They noted the following points:

- Knowledge of the wider context (economic, legal and socio-political).
- Knowledge of the firm.
- Training within the firm.
- Methodology for data analysis (needs of the firm, public demand, tools of analysis).
- Fulfilling the objectives of the training plan.
- Problems of training management.
- Formulating and initiating action.
- Conducting training courses (social relations and instrumental aspects).
- Staff development.
- Problems of control and management.

Of course all of these points cannot be covered by all training organisations. They serve only as a basis for analysis. Similarly Foudriat lists the following headings in his analysis of universities:

- Analysis of needs, training plan, training strategy, objectives.
- Evaluation.
- Legal, socio-economic and institutional contexts of continuing training.
- Knowledge of the firm.
- Pedagogy.
- Social psychology.
- Theories of learning and of education.
- Sociology.
- History of education.
- Philosophy of education.
- Teaching methods.
- Methodology and techniques of research.

As can be seen, a theoretical approach seems to feature more prominently in university courses. However, it is not necessary, in our opinion, in comparing the different kinds of training to take content alone into account. In effect, one often finds, in the very nature of things, the same kind of headings. Differences in this respect do not seem very significant. Much more important are differences in pedagogy, reflected by the respective weight accorded to lecture courses, to individual and collective research, projects, practical professional placements, etc.

CONCLUSIONS

Throughout this brief study, what might have struck the reader is the diversity of the situation in France, from the activism of popular education to the training specialism of the firm, where the emphasis swings between education and human resource management. To this diversity could be added the lack of a clearly defined status for the trainer and the highly differentiated functions of the adult educators.

These characteristics find reflection in the different types of training which correspond to them. In fact, the problem of adult education and that of the training of adult educators is not always posed in all its possible aspects. To do so would be like trying to explain the varied character of the French landscape itself.

As for the future of training of adult educators in France,

it is difficult once again to draw an overall picture:

- As far as training courses in firms are concerned, it seems that their significance will increase for economic reasons.
- Similarly in the case of *animateurs* of third-age activities, for demographic reasons.
- On the other hand, the socio-cultural *animateurs* are very vulnerable to the fluctuations of national and local politics in the cultural field.
- In the case of youth trainers, it is hard to predict the extent to which the projects in which they are involved will be maintained in their present forms.

Once again, therefore, we are in an uncertain situation, and it would appear difficult at this stage in the development of adult education in France to envisage much change taking place in the established practices and institutions.

BIBLIOGRAPHY

Ballier, A. and Lambert, J. (1974) *'L'Offre de formation de formateurs sur le marché de la formation', Education Permanante* no 23 (March-April).

Besnard, P. (1981) 'Metiér animateur', *L'Education* (19 February).

Caceres, B. (ed) (1985) *Guide de l'Education Populaire*, La Découverte.

Foudriat, M. (1986) *Les Formations de Formateurs dans les Universités*, Paris: Publications de la Sorbonne.

Lapassade, G. (1963) *L'Entrée dans la Vie. Essai sur l'inachèvement de l'homme*, Editions de Minuit.

Schwartz, B. (1981) *L'Insertion Professionelle et Sociale des Jeunes: rapport au Premier Ministre*, Paris: La Documentation Française.

7 Training adult educators in Greece

Dimitris Vergidis

In order to understand the training of adult educators in Greece, it is first necessary to understand the system of adult education in Greece. Therefore, the first section of this chapter will outline the institutions of continuing education.

THE INSTITUTIONS OF CONTINUING EDUCATION

Continuing education in Greece is organised by a number of different ministries, public organisations and private institutions. The main ones are discussed below, although those which work with the public services are omitted:

Public administration and continuing education

There is a General Secretariat for Popular Education within the Ministry of Culture. The Ministry of Agriculture also has centres for training in agriculture, runs courses about the application of agriculture and practical courses for women in agricultural areas. Finally, the Ministry of Labour has a Manpower Employment Organisation (OAED) which is concerned with apprenticeship and also with accelerated training schools. In addition, it has centres for young working men and young working women.

Private corporate bodies having responsibility to a ministry

There are a number of private organisations which offer courses for adults and young adults which have responsibility to one or other of the government departments. These organisations include: the National Youth Foundation, the National Welfare Organisation and the Greek Organisation for Small and Medium-Sized Enterprises and Handicrafts (EOMMEX).

The private sector and continuing education

This group may be divided into two sets of organisations: those which are private profit-making educational organisations and those foundations which are non-profit making and more publicly minded agencies, such as: the Greek Centre of Productivity (ELKEPA), the Greek Society for Business Administration (EEDE), the Greek Society for Operational Research (EEEE) and the Research and Self Education Centre (KEMEA).

Trades unions and co-operative bodies

There are two major organisations under this heading: the Centre for Study, Documentation and Training (KEMETE) and the School for the Training of Agricultural Co-operative Officials (PASEGES).

Continuing education in Greece virtually started at the beginning of the 1950s, as a response to the increased demand for a specialised work-force, created by the post-war economic growth and the one-dimensional school system which was orientated exclusively towards a general education — to the detriment of a technico-professional one. However, at the same time, it should be stressed that institutions of continuing education, in particular in agricultural areas, i.e. Adult Education and the National Welfare Organisation, had a specific ideological orientation aimed at the control and manipulation of the agricultural population. During recent years the increased demand for greater productivity both in industry and in the service sector, the restructuring of agriculture and entry into the European Economic Community, with the subsequent finances gained through the European Social Fund, have strongly contributed to the reshaping, broadening and improvement of continuing education in Greece.

THE ADULT EDUCATORS

The majority of adult educators are paid on an hourly basis and we may divide them into two categories:

(a) Adult educators who are teaching in fields related to their higher education level of studies, such as economics, sociology, agriculture, foreign languages, etc.

(b) Adult educators teaching in fields in which they have acquired a practical knowledge gained through their professional experience, such as dress-making, embroidery, popular art, etc.

As far as the first category of adult educators are concerned we may note the following:

1   Higher education in Greece has no connection with adult education. At the present time, for instance, departments of education in universities do not offer courses in adult education, so that students graduate without knowledge of specific adult education issues. Of course, law no 1268 (1982) on 'The Structure and Function of Higher Education' foresees that institutions of higher education must contribute to the development of continuing education (bill no 1268/82, article 11 § 3). At present this aim has not been achieved and the intention remains theoretical.
2   As already indicated the majority of adult educators are paid by the hour and they also teach part-time, their courses tend not to be adapted to the level and interests of their students and courses are usually theoretical without any connection to local problems or to the needs of students; consequently the educational value of these courses is questionable.
3   The pedagogical training of adult educators is confronted with difficulties because of their working status, and also their ignorance and negative attitudes towards teaching groups of adult students. They usually appear to prefer lecturing, thereby continuing the authoritarian pedagogical methods of the school.

On the other hand, adult educators, whose knowledge is based on professional experience have better contacts with students, but they are also confronted with other types of problem.

1   Adult educators in this category seem to limit their teaching to a very simplified approach to practical knowledge. They are, unfortunately, not able to adapt their teaching to the interests and the needs of their students, having a limited and fragmented knowledge of the subject. They lack the professional specialisation of being able to articulate practical and theoretical knowledge, which would enrich and develop the content of their courses.
2   Therefore, practical knowledge is not connected with its socio-economic and cultural context. For instance, dress-

making is directly related to fashion, but this does not mean that it should change every year. The view of society that clothes are useless from one year to another is not a practical view; we discard them not because they are worn out but because the are out of fashion. Adult educators in dress-making classes are seldom able to develop and analyse such issues, so that they lose the opportunity to develop a deeper understanding of their craft.

I must, of course, specify that there are many differences between the institutions of continuing education, so that the working conditions and training of adult educators varies. But in general the problems mentioned above concern the majority of adult educators who work in them.

POPULAR EDUCATION

It would be a very difficult task to discuss and develop, in these few pages, all the continuing education programmes offered in the country. I shall, therefore, limit myself to an analysis and interpretation of the facts of popular education. This form of education was established in 1943 (law no 837) but it did not become effective until 1951 when the relevant department was created in the Ministry of Education.

In 1954, bill no 3094 was passed. It concerned the fight against illiteracy and as a result a 'Central Committee Against Illiteracy' was created (renamed in 1965 as the Central Committee for Popular Education), having as its president the Minister of Education, and as secretary the executive in charge of the Department of Popular Education. Resulting from the same bill, County Committees against Illiteracy were created, which were renamed County Committees for Popular Education in 1965. They assumed responsibility for the foundation and organisation for night schools for adults.

Since 1976, popular education has been included in the context of a more general governmental policy for better education. More precisely, the popular education conferences that were until 1975-6 the main form of adult education were replaced by courses. Simultaneously the number of night schools has decreased, with very few existing at the present time. In 1981, as shown in Table 7.1, the amount of teaching sections multiplied itself by four in 1981 compared to 1979-80, while the number of hourly courses increased sixfold. The extension of teaching sections is due to an extremely ambitious programme,

Table 7.1 Development of the number of sections and teaching hours

Years	No of sections	Teaching hours	Average of hours by section
1976-7	2,733	94,969	34.7
1977-8	2,988	117,467	39.0
1978-9	3,272	132,185	40.0
1979-80	3,211	129,991	40.5
1981	14,044	766,380	54.6
1982	16,398	1,043,014	63.6
1983 (First semester)	7,548	538,413	71.3
1984 (First semester)	9,235	745,158	80.7

Source: Official Records – Ministry of Education. Direction for Adult Education, Athens 1977, 1978, 1979, 1980, 1981, and data analyses from Statistical Department
Note: A section is a group of participants and a teaching hour is fifty minutes teaching time.

55 per cent funded from the European Social Fund. But this has had some negative side-effects, such as institutions expanding without the proper structure or employing the appropriate number of educators.

This sudden increase in educational programmes without any planning has created many problems, so that towards the end of 1981 the Ministry established a committee whose duty it was to establish a new statute which would provide for the re-organisation and re-orientation of the institution. According to this new statute for popular education, enforced from the end of 1982:

1 The committee for each county for popular education has to be restructured in the following manner; it should include representatives from the main educational institutions in each county, as well as representatives from the trades unions and the local authorities.
2 In every county a Council for Popular Education, composed of professionals whose duty it is to develop educational programmes, is concerned with structural improvements and with the hiring of adult educators.
3 The free development of the students' personality must be encouraged in adult education, which includes the active participation in the social, economic and cultural events in each province.

The tremendous increase in educational programmes in 1981 has, however, created a situation which is difficult to alter despite all the efforts that have been made. It will be noted in Table 7.1 that the number of teaching sections decreased in 1983 but the increase in 1984 means that there is no opportunity to improve the quality of the provision. By contrast, it has also to be recognised that the duration of courses has doubled from 1979–80 to 1984, and we can say that as the average length of courses has increased this is a significant contributing factor to the improvement in popular education.

The 1983 programme specifies that the principal aim of popular education has nothing to do with the increase in quantity but, on the contrary, it is concerned with the problems that have been observed, specifying that the 1983 programme should:

• Renew and improve the content of adult education and its connection with economic and social issues.
• Create applicable experimental educational programmes.
• Emphasise the issues relating to the unemployment of young adults and women.
• Emphasise the training of staff and adult educators in order to achieve the other goals.

THE EDUCATION OF POPULAR EDUCATORS

It is important first to examine some statistical data that relate to popular education. It will be seen in Table 7.2 that in 1976 there were 1,940 people employed in popular education and that by 1981 the figure had dropped to 1,472 despite the fact that as Table 7.1 shows there was an increase in both the number of courses and teaching hours. Simultaneously, the average number of teaching sections and teaching hours for every educator (see Table 7.3) shows a steady increase, dramatically so in 1981. In 1981 the average number of teaching sections per adult educator had multiplied by 6.8 times from 1976–7, while the teaching hours for the same period had increased 10.6 times.

Five years after the decisive changes in adult education provision from conferences and night schools to the organisation of teaching sections, there has been a move towards the professionalisation of adult education, which has also provided a necessary component in the organisation of a systematic programme for the training of adult educators.

Table 7.2 Number of adult educators classified by occupation (1976-81)

Occupation	Number of adult educators									
	1976-7		1977-78		1978-79		1979-80		1981	
	No	%	No	%	No	%	No	%	No	%
School teachers	513	26.4	375	23.2	307	18.9	253	16.7	101	6.8
Professors	273	14.1	240	14.8	246	15.1	231	15.2	122	8.3
Others	63	3.3	57	3.5	71	4.4	56	3.7	51	3.5
Sub-total	849	43.8	672	41.5	624	38.4	540	35.6	274	18.6
Public servants (except school teachers)										
Doctors/veterinarians/midwives	94	4.8	67	4.1	69	4.2	55	3.6	50	3.4
Agronomists	102	5.3	61	3.8	45	2.8	46	3.0	35	2.4
Others	148	7.6	105	6.5	93	5.7	104	6.9	61	4.1
Sub-total	344	17.7	233	14.4	207	12.7	205	13.5	146	9.9
Priests	37	1.9	29	1.8	41	2.5	43	2.8	7	0.5
Private individuals										
Seamstresses	194	10.0	210	13.0	207	12.7	228	15.0	401	27.2
Foreign-language teachers	117	6.0	125	7.7	119	7.3	118	7.8	122	8.3
Engineers and general technicians	96	5.0	100	6.2	129	8.0	141	9.3	64	4.4
Others	303	15.6	249	15.4	299	18.4	242	16.0	458	31.1
Sub-total	710	36.6	684	42.3	754	46.4	729	48.1	1,045	71.0
Total	1,940	100.0	1,618	100.0	1,626	100.0	1,517	100.0	1,472	100.0

Source: Ministry of Education and Religion (1982) *Annual Data*, Athens.

Table 7.3 Teaching sections and teaching hours per educator

Year	No of sections	Teaching hours
1976-7	1.4	49.0
1977-8	1.9	72.6
1978-9	2.0	81.3
1979-80	2.1	85.7
1981	9.5	520.0

Source: Data provided by Ministry of Education, Direction for Adult Education, Athens, 1977, 1978, 1979, 1980, 1981.

We must also point out, as Table 7.2 shows, that in 1976-7, 44 per cent of adult educators were school teachers and only 37 per cent were private persons but by 1981 the proportion of teachers had dropped to 19 per cent and that of private individuals had risen to 71 per cent of the staff. This is an extremely important change in the composition of the adult educator's staff, due to the tremendous development of dress-making and embroidery courses, and confirms the trend of employing adult educators who have no other professional activity. By 1982, as Table 7.4 shows, there were 23 per cent of the total teaching force involved in these areas while only 14 per cent of those employed in adult education were school teachers. Indeed, Table 7.4 shows the breakdown of the teaching staff in adult education by occupation in 1982.

The trend to create full-time educators was strongly reinforced in the following years, but it proved difficult to train all educators in every field of popular education, so that the General Secretariat for Popular Education decided to focus upon the subjects that it considered to be of the most importance, based on the following criteria:

• Its relation to the five-year plan for economic and social development.
• Students' needs discussed in courses and popular meetings.
• Its relation to the general aims of popular education.

According to the above criteria the most important subjects appeared to be: co-operatives, parent-child relationships, sexual equality, weaving and computer science. Therefore, in the

Table 7.4 Adult educators classified according to occupation in 1982

Occupation	%	Total (%)
Public servants employed by the Ministry of Education		14.1
Professors (university/college)	0.37	
High-school teachers	9.00	
Primary/nursery school teachers	3.57	
Professional/lower technical/ and medium school teachers	0.71	
Others	0.45	
Public servants employed by other ministries		7.6
Doctors/veterinarians/midwives	1.95	
Lawyers/economists	0.33	
Agronomists/foresters	1.60	
Tourist industry workers	0.01	
Agricultural workers	0.67	
Social workers	0.31	
Engineers/technicians	0.38	
Archaeologists	0.06	
Military/police	0.31	
Others	1.98	
Priests	0.80	0.80
Non-public servants		77.5
Doctors/veterinarians/midwives	0.93	
Lawyers/economists	1.37	
Physicists, chemists, mathematicians	1.63	
Literature professors, theologians/teachers	1.03	
Writers/journalists	0.07	
Artists	9.96	
Engineers/technicians	3.50	
Foreign-language teachers	9.29	
Seamstresses	22.87	
Others	26.85	

Source: Ministry of Education, Direction for Adult Education (1982) *Data Analysis*, Athens.

context of an experimental programme, educators in the above subjects were selected through state examinations in eight of the country's fifty-two counties and they were placed on a special staff list having the following specifications:

- Specialisation in the subjects for which they were selected.
- Increase of their hourly fees by 50 per cent.
- Payment for up to thirty hours a month for preparation.
- Priority in establishing research programmes in subjects connected with popular education.

These special educators are expected to attend educational seminars, not only in their specialised fields but in more general subjects connected with popular education, such as teaching methods. Gradually, therefore, a staff of professional adult educators is being trained in the most important subjects, i.e. those who know both their subjects and also are familiar with teaching skills appropriate to adults.

TRAINING OF ADULT EDUCATORS

The 1983 educational programme specifies that 'The first and more fundamental step in order to develop popular education . . . is the training of its personnel' (Data Analysis, Ministry of Education, Direction of Adult Education 1982: 10). Consequently the request to the European Social Fund for 55 per cent financing was both for the educational programme and for the adult educators. The programme envisaged:

- Training 350 members of the popular education councils.
- Training 1,600 adult educators, responsible for educational centres and for members of popular education county committees.
- Training 350 adult educators in charge of special programmes.

A year later, in 1984, a further request was made to the Fund for financing a programme training 1,000 adult educators after having observed that most of the adult educators lacked pedagogical knowledge and professional specialisation. More precisely, the 1984 programme planned for educational seminars for 500 adults educators and further professional practical training for another 500.

According to the data from the General Secretariat for Popular Education, see Table 7.5, over eighty seminars for adult education personnel and educators occurred in 1983 and during the first semester of 1984.

Table 7.5 Number of seminars for adult educators and adult education personnel

Year	Seminars No	Participants No	Duration No of days	Participants Average no	Average duration No of days
1983	39	3,611	205	92.6	5.3
1984 (first semester)	44	3,102	159	70.5	3.6

Source: General Secretariat for Popular Education, Statistic Department

In Table 7.5 we can see that there were approximately 6,700 participants, adult educators and officials, at these training seminars, many more than the 1,500, approximately, who worked as adult educators in 1981. However, we must point out that this large increase cannot be justified only by the increase in amount of educational provision (see Table 7.1).

These are, of course, very informative short seminars aiming to highlight the goals of popular education and to provide some elementary knowledge of pedagogy. They are not considered to be systematic nor organised pedagogical training. On the other hand, data analyses do indicate that participation dropped from 92.6 per seminar in 1983 to 70.5 in the first part of 1984, a positive finding given the right circumstances. However, the average length of the seminar also fell, from 5.3 days to 3.6 days. The longest seminars were organised for members of the councils for popular education and each lasted for two weeks.

The large attendance and length of the first seminars can be explained firstly by interest and, perhaps, enthusiasm that popular education evokes but, secondly, by staff turnover. The institution of popular education did not, however, take advantage of the initial interest shown by the participants in those early seminars. Hence, we discover in the 1985 programme that most educators lacked educational training and professional qualifications, so that their teaching has not adapted to the ideals of adult education that require 'personal growth and development of the participants'. Simultaneously, it was noted by the General Secretariat for Popular Education in 1985 in its request to the European Social Fund that 'the level of the adult education does not meet the actual demands of the labour market'.

However, the 1985 programme included the training of 1,000

adult educators, also financed by a 55 per cent grant from the European Social Fund, but the results of the efforts have not proved satisfactory. Therefore, in 1986 the General Secretariat for Popular Education decided to organise the experimental programme which was to choose and train educators in specialised fields — as was discussed earlier. Finally, the Department of Planning and Training of Educators of the General Secretariat for Popular Education has included in its own special programme about 100 adult educators, who are now attending advanced seminars.

It seems, however, that the increased amount of training of adult educators between 1983 and 1985 proved to be detrimental to the quality of the training programme except, of course, for the few seminars which were properly organised. Hence the choice and training of adult educators on a smaller scale seems to be a necessary step in order to improve the infrastructure and to increase the quality of seminars.

We must add that the General Secretariat for Popular Education has in the past collaborated with the Research and Self-Education Centre (KEMEA) in organising training seminars for educators, and specifically for members of the Councils of Popular Education. KEMEA, itself, has the following aims:

- To participate in people's education, particularly for lower social classes, with modern pedagogical methods.
- To develop the creative potential of its participants and their active participation in all levels of social activities.
- To study and analyse social issues.
- To eliminate the monologue and authoritarian methods in adult education and to promote 'self-education'.

This organisation also receives funding from the European Social Fund for long-term training programmes for small groups of adult educators, so that they can be hired by public or private institutions as adult educators.

CONCLUSIONS

One of the main obstacles in Greece to the improvement of popular educational programmes is the lack of adult educators with professional qualifications and teacher training. Despite the extensive growth of continuing education and the fact that the political authorities realise its potential in economic, social and cultural terms, no effort has been made until the present time to establish a systematic training programme for adult educators and, regrettably, there are no plans for the future. The result of this is that the lack of training encourages those who teach adults to employ authoritarian teaching methods which do not allow for the participants to experience personal growth and development. This might account for the low level of adult education provision. More precisely, as adult educators have no basic knowledge of teaching methods, they cannot apply the principles of adult education, they are unable to work in small groups and do not understand the principles of group dynamics, which results in the more traditional school type of approach to teaching, i.e. lecturing, rigidly prepared methods, etc. Hence, this is off-putting to potential participants.

It is also important to remind ourselves that most adult educators are paid by the hour and many have another form of employment so that the profession of adult education is still in the making in Greece. Its social function, professional training, necessity and public recognition have still to be determined.

Finally, the systematic training of adult educators, both in teaching methods and professional specialisation, requires the universities to co-operate with the institutions of continuing education. It also requires the training of professional adult educators who will be responsible for the main educational programmes and will also be concerned with improving the quality of adult education in Greece.

BIBLIOGRAPHY

General Secretariat for Popular Education (ed.) (1985) *Decentralisation and Popular Education: the participation of adult educators in local development* (3rd international seminar. Yannena, 6-8 October 1983 directed by Maria Eliou.) Athens: General Secretariat for Popular Education.

— (1981) *Continuing Education in Greece*, Athens: Society for Labour Studies.

General Secretariat for Popular Education (ed.) (1985) *Texts on Popular Education*, Athens.

Demunter, P., Varnave-Scoura, G. and Vergidis, D. (1984) 'L'éducation populaire en Grèce', *Edition par les cahiers d'étude du C.U.E.E.P.* no 1 Jan.

Demunter, P. (1984) *La Formation des formateurs d'adultes*, FUNOC.

Vergidis, D. (1985) 'Continuing Education in Greece in the Context of Popular Education', *Pedagogical Sciences* (8th vol) Athens.

Vergidis, D. (1985) *Teacher Training and Local Cultural Development*, Volos: International Symposium on 'The New Directions in Pedagogical Studies', 25-27 Sept.

8 The organisation of agencies for adult education in Italy

Paolo Federighi
translated by Pam Denicolo (University of Surrey)

ADULT EDUCATION AGENCIES IN THE ITALIAN SYSTEM

Adult education in Italy

At present, Italy has no national law with respect to the education of adults. This situation acts as an obstacle to those intending to observe or describe Italian adult education. The absence of such a law does not imply that there are no agencies, organisations or an infrastructure. All these exist but in a diffused form which is difficult to control. Each public body (local, regional or national) is competent in this field, taking adult education into account in their planning and budgeting. None of these public bodies has by law, however, precise responsibility in this area.

Numerous private organisations, which might come from associations of any kind, are actually practising the education of adults. In addition to political, trade union, co-operative, cultural and religious organisations, there are private organisations which practise it as a commercial venture.

In the field of formal education, the Italian system is extremely weak. In effect, formal education is limited to basic levels and professional training occurs for only a small group. As far as the instructional field is concerned, adult education is offered to only 0.3 per cent of the potential market. The majority of instruction available might be categorised as non-formal liberal adult education. In this sector private organisations, rather than public providers of education, prevail in terms of realising financial opportunities and availing themselves of human and material resources. Access to non-formal education is primarily mediated through membership of these organisations, so that it is restricted to a limited, privileged sector of the population.

Taxonomy of adult education providers

In order to gain a perspective on this fragmented situation we have chosen a definition of adult education which conforms to that which was produced by UNESCO at its Nairobi Conference in 1976. This definition allows us to abandon the image of adult education which restricts it to the old 'education of the populace' model and to consider, from an educational perspective, all those organisations and activities which, in fact, operate in the field of formal and non-formal adult education. This definition specifies that

> The term 'adult education' denotes the entire body of organized educational processes, whatever the content, level and method, whether formal or otherwise, whether they prolong or replace initial education in schools, colleges and universities, as well as in apprenticeship, whereby persons regarded as adult by the society to which they belong develop their abilities, enrich their knowledge, improve their technical or professional qualifications, or turn them in a new direction and bring about changes in their attitudes or behaviour in the two-fold perspective of full personal development and participation in balanced and independent, social, economic, and cultural development.

Starting from this definition, the cadre of organisations and public and private organisations which provide adult education is staffed by full-time, part-time or voluntary workers. It is organised as detailed below.

Private and public provision

1   Formal education: primary school, secondary school, high school, university.
2   Professional training: initial qualification, updating, specialisation, government-sponsored training.
3   Cultural education: libraries, film libraries, museums, concert halls, theatres, radio and television, cultural centres, provincial and local provisions, associational provision, foundations, sporting bodies.
4   Health education: hospitals, cottage hospitals, medical advice centres, mental health institutions, addiction clinics.
5   Social services education: community centres, senior citizens centres, prison service.

Private organisations and providers

In this sector there are many other providers of educational opportunities, including:

1 Political, trade unions and co-operative training are provided in classes organised by the political parties, trade unions, co-operatives and the feminist movement.
2 Cultural and recreational training are provided by national, regional and local cultural associations, research institutes, public refuge hostels, working men's clubs, cultural clubs. In addition, there is cinema, local and national radio and television.
3 Civic associations provide local committees and parents' associations.
4 Public assistance associations provide assistance for the elderly and for those who, for whatever reason, have become marginalised.

Quantitative elements

Research on the pattern of adult education provision and development

All that is available regarding the consistency of provision on a national scale are approximate statistics which cannot be verified. In the absence of a specific investigation at national level, it is preferable to extrapolate some quantitative elements of an actual research study which has taken place in Tuscany. This study set about considering, from a particular point of view, the diverse bodies — professional and voluntary — in the public and private infrastructure with different mandates which employ different methods but have either direct or indirect educational objectives.

The objectives of the research can be described thus:

1 To study the status, role and professionalism of the practitioners.
2 To try to define the best plan of study to train these practitioners to work in the diverse sectors of adult education.
3 To promote organisations whereby practitioners already in the system can contribute more strongly to innovations that are occurring than they can at present due to the divisions that currently exist.

4   To establish a process to reconstitute formal, non-formal and liberal education at the same level of permanency, so that future educational practitioners are not divided and isolated by age level, discipline or sector of intervention (function).

The first results

At the time of writing (1987) the research had been conducted in territories in seven of the nine provinces of Tuscany. There were about 4,000 practitioners but the results that are presented here consider only 652 practitioners working in five different urban areas, and these results can be treated as reliable.

In the area researched there were about 407,000 inhabitants, which means that there is approximately one practitioner for every 624 members of the population including children, although this figure is reduced to one practitioner for every 480 adult members of the population. If these data could be extrapolated into the national context, then there would be about 90,000 practising adult educators in Italy. However, there was a strong skew in this sample, with the tourist and industrial areas being strongly favoured, where the ratio was approximately one adult educator for every 370 adult inhabitants but in other urban areas the ratio was closer to one adult educator for every 627 adult members of the population. Because there is so much variation, it would be unwise to advance hypotheses about the national dimensions. However, these data allow for the conclusion to be drawn that there exists a strong distortion in different areas of the country, i.e. north-south, centre-suburbs, etc.

From the data collected in Tuscany some 51 per cent of the practitioners work in public organisations and 49 per cent in private companies. In addition, it was discovered that 39 per cent of the adult educators work for voluntary organisations. It was also possible to determine that some 32 per cent of the respondents were part-time and 29 per cent were full-time, but it was not possible to discover these data for the remainder. Only 8.7 per cent of those who work in the voluntary sector work full-time, with 60 per cent working in a voluntary capacity. It is perhaps significant that 18 per cent of those who work in the public sector are also volunteers. In that sector, however, full-time workers prevail — 44 per cent.

Taking these elements into account, particularly the large incidence of voluntary workers and the number of part-time practitioners, it is possible to understand the wide variety of professions to which practitioners belong, as Table 8.1 shows.

Table 8.1 Occupations from which adult educators are drawn in Tuscany

Occupation	%
Artisans	1.4
Artists	0.2
Civil servants	9.5
Clerics	2.7
Doctors	5.1
Educationalists	2.0
Health workers	1.0
Housewives	0.6
Librarians	5.1
Managers	0.6
Nurses	2.0
Office workers	10.5
Pensioners	1.7
Politicians	0.2
Psychiatrists	0.4
Psychologists	2.9
Researchers	0.2
Retailers	0.6
Self-employed	0.6
Social workers	5.3
Students	7.3
Teachers	31.4
Technicians	1.4
Trade unionists	0.4
Unemployed	1.6
Unskilled workers	0.6
Others	4.7

The first important point that emerges from Table 8.1 is that adult education is not only the prerogative of the professionals. Additionally, it must be pointed out that there are manual workers amongst the practitioners although these make up less than 10 per cent of the total, and of these only seven (out of 100) have found a position in organisations of a public nature. Above all, it is mainly in the civic associations that manual workers have a role to play in the education of adults.

From the research it seems that the prevailing functions performed by the organisations in which the practitioners work are those listed in Table 8.2.

Table 8.2 Occupational area of adult educators

Occupational area	%
Cultural activities	25.5
Health	8.5
Professional training of adults	13.4
Social security	14.8
Teaching adults	22.2
Other	15.6

Note: In the category 'other' are included organisations with a variety of functions, including those of leisure.

PLACES OF TRAINING FOR ADULT EDUCATORS

Responsibility for training adult education practitioners falls on colleges of higher education, public organisations, particularly those involved in development programmes and civic associations.

Colleges of higher education

Colleges of higher education provide two kinds of preparation: the first, at university, is mainly the basic/initial training of practitioners and the second, in the professional schools with undergraduate courses, provides mainly specialist training in the art of teaching. The former can be found in the universities of Arezzo, Cosenza, Florence, Rome, Padova and Palermo, where the students have the opportunity to study the theory, history and methodology of adult education. The teaching of adult education was recently introduced into the Italian universities by the implementation of a course at the University of Florence in 1969 and then at the University of Rome in the same year, and this was followed by courses in the other universities.

In 1967, a course was started at the Centre for Professional Education for Social Workers (CEPAS) at the University of Rome and also at other schools for social workers. At the present time, however, there is a trend to close these courses in the schools.

The second type of preparation is being developed in schools for librarians, experts in communication systems, museologists, psychologists, sociologists and social workers. Recently adult education has been included in the syllabus of degree courses for cultural heritage at the universities of Viterbo and Udine.

Public organisations

Over and above the basic school and university system, public interventions in the training of practitioners are promoted in (i) the teaching sectors of regional institutes for educational research, experimentation and updating, (ii) the professional training sector of regional administrations and also in other public bodies, and (iii) the sector for liberal educational activities of all educational and cultural agencies, although this is often intermittent rather than through a specific programme of preparation.

Civic associations

Courses and seminars are also organised by the civic associations, political party schools and the schools organised by the trade unions and cultural associations. On the initiative of cultural associations, there have been established centres for the training of adult educators. Although not active today, the initiative of the Centro di Sermoneta and the Humanitarian Society (based in Meina) have contributed a great deal in the past to formative activities for practitioners of adult education.

PATTERN OF TRAINING IN ADULT EDUCATION

University training

There are no degree courses in adult education in Italian universities. It follows that there is no officially determined university curriculum or certification for practitioners of adult education. There is only the opportunity, as indicated earlier, of following a course within a degree programme of another discipline.

In Italy, the University of Florence has the largest number of students following a course in adult education. Each year 300 students are examined in the discipline and ten students discuss it in their doctoral dissertations. Training in the university is achieved by a strict balance between research, didactics and the problems of society. Teaching is organised on the basis of fundamental principles thus: (a) the university should not be independent of society but should be integrated with it, (b) theoretical arguments are not borne from the discipline, but are derived from the articulation of a scientific paradigm in relation to present reality, (c) the educational agent responsible is the body of students manifesting themselves as society within the university and the university within the larger society, (d) study is formulated in research and training.

The most productive and consequential method of study is the seminar workshop, which focuses on precise projects given to the university by local administration, other associations and the cultural infrastructure, etc.

Academics, and also the students, study adult education by practising it. They develop research and interventions for the most urgent problems presented by society. Students studying adult education take an active part in research activities, e.g. research on 'Organisations and Activities of Adult Education in Tuscany', evaluation of courses such as the '150 hour' programme, research and experimentation on the educational development function of the public library at Castelfiorentino, constructing an urban system of education for adults in the borough of Prato.

Training at the local level

During the past few years some local organisations have started to confront the problem of training practitioners. In some cases, they provide suitable offices and centres where the following activities usually occur: documentation and the production of materials, lease of resource centre, provision of public information on activities, basic and specialised training of practitioners. These training initiatives are, however, limited and have not produced precisely organised models. In spite of this, an overview is attempted here of some of the principal topics which occur in these formative activities. They can be divided into two groups: the first examines some of the basic techniques — programme planning, educational management, educational providers, documentation and publicity and the role of the adult educator; the second includes study of a variety of aspects of the role — methods in educational research, techniques in facilitating adult learning, audio-visual aids, field trips, adult education and

Table 8.3 The highest educational level of adult educators in Tuscany

Level	%
Primary school	0.6
Secondary school	3.5
High school	42.0
Specialist diploma	6.8
Graduate	46.7
Post-graduate	0.4

libraries and museums, the use of music and festivals and also adult education in ecology, health education, etc.

Training of practitioners within associations

In associations, training is conducted without precise formative strategies. There is no sense in which problems which practitioners might encounter are anticipated and preventative training offered. All training is developed in an on-going manner. At times, when confronted with problems which occur in the normal running of the organisation, formative and finalised programmes of training are organised but this is usually only undertaken for the most urgent problems and in the most general manner. In fact, the organised training of practitioners in these associations has a very casual and disjointed character. Depending upon chance and opportunity, new additions are made to the curriculum as appropriate.

A synthesis of the main formative problems incurred in the associations' formative training of practitioners can be discovered in an examination of any of the following fields: organisational aims, objectives methods and functions within the wider society; inter-relationship between the organisations and the wider society; the organisation, its workforce and the wider public.

EDUCATIONAL CONDITIONS OF PRACTITIONERS

The research conducted in Tuscany demonstrates that the practitioners' levels of education are medium/high. Ninety-six per cent have attended high school, with about 50 per cent being graduates. Table 8.3 provides data about the educators of adults.

To have a certificate in higher education is not, however, an absolute indicator of perfect formative ability, and the general data reveal a lack of initial training in the field of adult education. Furthermore, the initial training received at school and at university has not necessarily resulted in employment opportunities occurring. It is also significant that over 50 per cent of the practitioners consider school or university to have been of little or no relevance in developing their own abilities in adult education; much more importance is attributed to experience in work and their participation in different associations. In a number of cases, however, training in the specialist field, e.g. cinema, library, has been more useful than an initial basic training in adult education. In addition, practitioners employed in the public infrastructural organisations of society who have followed the appropriate courses of study are in a similar position in regard to adult education training; in fact, their training is left until they are in the workplace where they are then trained according to their needs. Of course, it is well known that this form of training results in cultural and social reproduction.

It must also be noted that regular updating is not accessible to everybody; work contracts that regulate the activities of different practitioners do not always specify the possibility of study leave, even when the work is not remunerated. Therefore, the practitioners' training occurs at the place of work, through 'natural' and non-organised processes. It is significant that only 31 per cent of the practitioners had, during their working life, taken part in a training course and only 23.3 per cent had participated in a seminar.

A LAW TO OVERCOME THE PRESENT CONDITIONS

Whether the field is formal or non-formal adult education, there is no curriculum that ensures professionalism of practice. In instruction and educational and other activities, teachers or librarians, for example, proceed by a mixture of intuition and trial and error. Only the high level of practitioner motivation and specialist preparation in their field allows them to achieve a high standard in the education of adults. In order to overcome this problem and to establish a high level of professionalism in adult education a number of initiatives must be taken that do not yet exist in Italy. These would include: departments and graduate courses to be established in the universities; residential centres to be established for in-service training of practitioners. In order to achieve these and other innovations a law should be implemented in Italy that gives people the right to adult education training. This would lay the institutional foundations necessary to cope with problems of status, role and professionalism of the practitioners. Indeed, in 1987 the Italian Association for Adult Education proposed that a law should be passed to deal with this problem, another section of which should outline new conditions for practitioners. However, for such a law to become a reality, three separate bodies are envisaged.

1   An adult education body to be established to manage the provisions of the law, whether central, regional, provincial or local adminstration. Basically this is to apply the law and co-ordinate its implementation at an executive level. Its competence should be in both general (formal and liberal education) and specific (abiding by the law and its dictates) throughout Italy.
2   That a body for formal adult education should be established, with a distinct role for education in the field of work, i.e. nursery, primary, secondary and high school. This body should have a five-year lifespan in order to develop the work of adult education.
3   A body should be established for liberal adult education. As far as the public sector is concerned, provision should be made for the specialist requirements in whatsoever area they operate, e.g. museums, libraries. In the private sector, the only activities that should be managed are those which lead to the training of adult educators, and then this should only occur at the request of the private sector.

As far as on-going education and re-training is concerned, the proposed law makes provision for four areas of initiation:

1   The training of trainers for the specialisation and updating of practitioners.
2   The development of adult education in universities.
3   The specialisation and re-training of practitioners who are already in service in formal and liberal education.
4   The training, updating and retraining and specialisation of practitioners in cultural and educational associations.

CONCLUSION

The training of practitioners constitutes one of the most important fields in the development of international co-operation. This is particularly relevant for European countries where, despite innumerable difficulties, attempts are being made to create the new 'European person'. Emigrants were the first people to make this possible and now it is necessary to develop the practitioners' ability to contribute to these now formative training processes which have, until now, been only ephemeral and restricted to such phenomena as international cultural exchanges. It is a challenge for adult education to study and predict solutions applicable and practicable to the time and task, which at present appear to be little more than a mirage. The idea of giving life to a European university for adult education is a part of this dream, but if it were to be realised then there would be the opportunity of training new practitioners for transnational adult education for the third millennium.

However, these ideas will remain at the level of aspiration unless practical steps can be taken so as to make progress. In order to prepare practitioners for this new world, it is necessary to transform the method of training, so that the role of education is not seen to be merely reproductive but also creative and innovative. This process has to be started with adults, from their present problems and milieux. Solutions have to be found which respond to collective needs and are arrived at by testing all ideas that emerge from formative situations in order to produce results that will lead to new diverse social and economic realities.

9 Training of adult educators in Spain

José Quintana Cabanas and José Valcárcel Amador

This chapter falls into two parts: the first examines the training of adult educators in the state sector and was written by José Quintana whilst the second part was written by José Valcárcel and focuses on the private sector.

THE PREPARATION OF ADULT EDUCATORS IN THE STATE SECTOR

It is both suitable and convenient to sub-divide this section of Spanish adult education into two forms: the non-regulated and the regulated. The former comprises both non-formal adult education, i.e. correspondence courses, professional training, popular universities, etc. and alternative forms of adult education, i.e. socio-cultural activities, participation research, etc. By contrast, regulated adult education is that system which provides training for adults at the same level as for children and then results in the same qualifications being awarded. However, in this latter instance, it is provided for adults unable to benefit from the normal school provision, for whatever reason. Hence, regulated adult education consists of literacy and primary education, both rudimentary scholarship for new readers and basic general education (EGB). These may be followed by secondary and further education as in the normal system, although there are some special adult modes, e.g. Instituto Nacional de Bachillerato a Distancia (INBAD).

A significant point arising here is that since the EGB refers to a kind of primary education, the Spanish law requires educators who teach adults at this level to be trained primary-school teachers.

The approach of the Ministry of Science and Education towards adult education in recent decades should be in order to understand both the role of the teacher of adults and also the training each requires. During the period of industrial

115

development in the 1960s it was necessary to reduce illiteracy in order to create a qualified workforce. An official decree, in August 1963, established the Adult Literacy Campaign, and in 1970 the General Education Act considered the necessity of *educación permanente* for adults and specified an objective of allowing adults to acquire an academic degree. Consequently, in 1973 the Adult Literacy Campaign was officially ended and the Permanent Adult Education Programme (EPA) was introduced with an initial staff of 1,000 teachers and with different educational institutions contributing to the programme, each of which were allocated additional staff.

EPA teachers must have EGB teacher training, i.e. an initial university education. Some EGB teacher training colleges have considered creating programmes with special options, such as those for teachers of special education and teachers of infants and adults, but these have not yet been implemented. However, an EGB teacher who wishes to become an EPA teacher must specify this intention when he/she sits the entrance examination, or during the time he/she is teaching within the normal school system. In this latter instance, many teachers wish to be transferred to EPA so that they can work under more advantageous conditions, both in respect to location and to timetable.

However, the need for specific teacher training that would equip them to work with adults has not been specifically stated, although in some instances they may have actually undertaken courses in literacy. Nevertheless some initiatives have been taken in this respect:

1 Institutes of continuing education in some universities have organised training courses for teachers of adults.
2 Some private institutions, such as the permanent Workers' Education Service (SEPT) in Barcelona, have provided more or less complete courses.
3 Some summer-school programmes have included adult education training opportunities.
4 EPA groups have organised their own training, e.g. between 1975 and 1980 the Madrid Inspectorate organised some seminars about having an academic degree in adult education.
5 Some Spanish universities' departments of pedagogy have offered programmes in this subject, recognising the social responsibility underlying the practice of adult education, e.g. that at Seville.

A case study might be that of the Pontifical University at

Salamanca, where the Advanced School for Adult Training (ESEFA) has been established since 25 May 1966 and which has recently extended its activities to include that of social *animation*. Besides *animateurs*, ESEFA intends to train qualified teachers of adults and specialists in adult education in order to promote adult education. In addition, the school is interested in starting a Documentation, Orientations and Research Centre. In regard to adult education at present, ESEFA has two levels: qualified teacher and expert. All candidates who wish to become qualified teachers must already be qualified EGB teachers, or students enrolled in EGB teacher training at a university college. Their programme of studies is:

Year 1

(a) History of adult pedagogy (andragogy) — both in Spain and abroad. This includes a study of both public and private organisations that have specialised in adult education.
(b) Psychology of adult development — including sexual, physical and attitudinal characteristics. This is in relation to family and work life and also in the sphere of social living. Axiology is also studied.
(c) Programme planning.

Year 2

(a) Teaching methods in adult education.
(b) Critical awareness and use of the social media.
(c) Adult learning and its educational implications.
(d) Educational technology.

It is also necessary to prepare a teaching practice diary and students also have to submit a dissertation about an area of adult education that they choose. On successful completion students are awarded a diploma in adult education. This award is only made to those who are already in possession of qualified teacher status and who are already university graduates.

Courses at ESEFA are intensive and require morning and evening attendance (full-time), and they also require both theoretical and practical elements.

The General Direction for Educational Promotion (MEC) has maintained, since 1984, that it is necessary to give teachers of adults an initial training that could lead to the creation of post-graduate courses of flexible duration, to which all teachers who have competed their first grade at university could have access. In addition, it is argued that there should be a second professional level of training which would include within the curriculum: andragogy, developmental psychology, methodology and other specialist options such as management of a centre and multi-media systems. The MEC, in conjunction with local government and other organisations, has encouraged a series of consultations and suggestions regarding the training of adult educators and has produced a report (1984) about it, in which it has recommended fifteen projects for adult education pedagogical renewal in various regions in the country.

Finally, the Barcelona University Autonomous Educational Sciences Sector is planning to commence a course in pedagogics in adult education for graduates and middle-grade technicians. In 1984, in collaboration with other organisations, they organised a course to train adult education teachers. Candidates were unemployed graduates and the plan was to prepare them to become teachers of adults. The course had three core subjects:

(a) Theory and history of adult education (non-formal, permanent, popular education, alternative adult education, literacy).
(b) Psychology of adult education (adulthood, adolescence, creativity, etc.).
(c) Sociology of adult education (social demands, policy about adult education, legislation, etc.).

Naturally the students also studied group dynamics.

This brief overview completes the study of the training of teachers of adults in the state sector of adult education. The preparation of adult educators in the private sector is reviewed below.

THE TRAINING OF TEACHERS OF ADULTS IN THE PRIVATE SECTOR

While there is a system of training in the state sector of adult education, it is harder to define and describe the role of an adult educator in the non-state sector.

As Professor Quintana points out above it is necessary for the teacher of adults at an official level to be an EGB teacher whose function is seen as that of transmitting knowledge. In contrast, the teacher of adults in the private sector seeks to motivate, animate and encourage the adult to develop his/her educational tasks in a continuous manner. However, these two approaches depict ideal types rather than provide a perfect reflection of reality. Teachers in the public sector do not submit to the rigid official curriculum and they do try to go beyond the specified programme imposed by the government, while teachers in the private sector are hardly dependent upon fixed rules and are creative and imaginative in their approach. But they confront financial difficulties that both interfere with and influence their work. Often these teachers do not receive sufficient financial reward to satisfy their most basic necessities, so that their influence is diminished both with their students and in their immediate locality.

It is necessary to unify both educational strands, i.e. concerning both the public- and the private-sector teacher, so that teachers of adults can be created who know how to provide an open and broad approach to the governmental directions, adapting them according to the circumstances of and in negotiation with their students.

It is essential that each teacher, or group of teachers, undertakes whatever job he or she wishes within his or her own abilities, so that new approaches are only commenced when they can be accomplished. Adult education must be made a respected and well-organised field, with untested practice and hasty improvisations abolished.

At the present time there are some new initiatives in Spain and experiments are being tried out with a new conception of the educator of adults; these are occurring in popular universities, working camps, schools for life and schools for socio-cultural *animateurs*. They are developing in the same way as in the official adult education provision, producing a new image of the adult educator.

Although adult education is now professionally demanding, it is only certificated by the diploma as an EGB teacher. It is necessary, therefore, to create a new qualification that assists the work, since there are an increasing number of professional groups, such as psychologists, sociologists and social workers who are starting upon this complex task without a clear idea of what it means to be a teacher of adults. There are very few programmes in Spain that offer appropriate teacher training. New teachers' centres are being established and this is an important step forward. They have been placed at a second level, and are not dependent upon the central administration, but upon the local government of the country. These centres are responsible for staff development in different pedagogical fields and constitute a significant alternative to preparation, not only for adult education but for the whole of the educational system.

In contrast to the state initiative, there are also certain groups which have expressed an interest in creating a mentors' school, or schools for teachers of adults. This would be a useful alternative to the substructure of popular education, so long as both experience and practice follow the direction that teacher education takes.

Part IV

German-speaking countries

10 Basic and further education and training for adult educators in Austria

Ursula Knitter-Lux
translated by Charles P. Hancock

Adult education in Austria is organised into a number of independent, non-statutory associations, often in competition with each other and certainly with less co-operation between them than could be desired. The eleven largest of these have their own approach to the education of their workers, including the leaders of individual courses.

FOLK HIGH SCHOOLS (*VOLKSHOCHSCHULEN* — VHS)

The Austrian folk high schools have the longest tradition of education of teachers and staff and, indeed, at the foundation of the Association of Austrian Folk High Schools (Verbande Osterreichische Volkshochschulen — VOV) the need to have properly prepared teachers was regarded as a priority. The VOV offers seminars for teachers, course leaders and directors of the folk high schools. For directors, there is an on-going conference programme; for course leaders there are three levels of seminar: introductory, on-going and problem-orientated; for teachers (and course leaders) there are two types of seminar — introductory and on-going. The three different forms of seminar are described below.

Introductory seminars

These are general seminars and they have several main purposes: the first, to make the new entrant into the profession aware of the role, function and educational-political orientation of the VHS; the second, to introduce the recruit to the problems of the adult learner; the third, to offer some understanding of special teaching methods for adult learners, including educational psychology and educational sociology; the fourth, to provide the beginner with some awareness of group dynamics and the

123

teaching of social interaction; the fifth, for each of the specific subject seminars to provide more detailed information about the planning and teaching of individual subjects.

In addition to these general aims these seminars have a number of specific objectives. The teacher will become competent enough to examine how far he/she and the course members are active co-workers and group members in the learning process and to what extent they are in agreement with the objectives, content and conduct of the course. This does not mean that the course leader should simply abandon his/her views and concepts in order, in a spurious appearance of democracy, to bow to the wishes of the majority (although the course leader must be influenced by the views of the students), but it does mean that the 'problematic needs' of all the group are the subject of real debate and discussion.

The teacher should understand the type of educational aims and objectives that are being sought and constantly bear these in mind during the planning of the course. The learning objectives may be defined in general as: the knowledge and skills that should be achieved during the course and the acquisition of the ability to demonstrate that these have been achieved.

The spread of these courses is very uneven, with only about twenty of them being arranged each year by the VOV in the whole of Austria, apart from Vienna. However, in Vienna alone there are approximately another forty-five seminars for course leaders. It is hoped that adult educators will participate in these courses and although they are free they are not a requirement for course leaders.

On-going seminars

General on-going seminars allow the possibility of a confrontation between the theoretical background and the personal experience of the teacher or course leader. In addition, subject-specific seminars offer the experienced course leader the possibility of both subject updating and also an opportunity to explore new or different teaching and learning approaches, including facilitation. Furthermore, their purpose is to encourage the teachers to consider their own attempts to develop and refine adult learning and teaching theories and to present them to colleagues with the intention of enhancing further their own roles as practical exponents of adult education theory.

Problem seminars

These seminars have another main function in as much as they are intended to examine the connection between the VHS and the problems that arise in the wider society, e.g. in political or economic institutions. In many instances, at the end of the seminars an action plan for either the VHS or a VHS association will be drawn up that will influence the future way in which the VHS will respond to a particular problem.

CATHOLIC ADULT EDUCATION TRAINING CENTRE

The Catholic Adult Education Training Centre has offered seminars to its workers for a number of years in various professional disciplines, e.g. librarians and teachers. In these training programmes both 'function-independent' and 'function-dependent' qualifications are worked towards. In the former, the objectives are understood to be: a concern with the spiritual life of the worker; the need to help the worker to 'work with him-/herself'; the struggle to create a place in daily life for contemplation, congregation and prayer in contrast to the increasing pressures of daily life. The inclusion of these basic values and beliefs is regarded as fundamental since they are seen to be at the heart of human individuality. Similarly, the development of an acceptable method of interaction between people, a dialogical relationship of equals, in an open and self-critical manner is regarded as being of importance.

In the latter, subjects are taught alongside those topics and skills that are connected more specifically with the course or role with which the worker is primarily concerned.

The training centre has its own educational concept and methods for workers in the community and public affairs work. Additionally, models of community-politics, cultural models and models of social welfare are also examined.

PEOPLE'S LIBRARIES

Adult education libraries in Austria have, despite the diversity of controlling organisations, developed a universally accepted staff training scheme. Since 1965, librarians who have found a position have been offered courses in training libraries. After an examination, a certificate from the training council is granted and although the state organisation for adult education has recommended that its members recognise this certificate and facilitate the training of librarians, there is no compulsion for them to do so. Until 1985, these courses were offered only in Vienna, Salzburg and Graz, so that librarians in the more remote country areas have been prevented from attending. However, in 1985 a distance-learning self-directed course was started with some face-to-face contact in block study at the Federal Institute of Adult Education at Strobl on Wolfgangsee. In addition, it is intended to ensure by state regulation that this group is better provided for in respect of its continuing education.

OCCUPATIONAL FURTHER EDUCATION INSTITUTIONS

This further education has in the main been conducted by two organisations, one representing the employers and the other the employees. Both attempt to ensure that the course leaders, who are almost all teachers, are given special instruction in the arts of teaching adults. These teacher training programmes are organised in nine 'problem circles' and the teaching is so arranged that each problem circle is covered in a single unit so that there is no compulsory course plan that must be followed. The nine problem circles are:

- Contact between students and teachers.
- Reduction in anxiety in adults about learning and overcoming learning difficulties.
- Educational aims and objectives; stages of learning.
- Lesson planning.
- Speech training for teaching and the lecture.
- Learning through play.
- Use of audio-visual aids.
- Group work.
- Evaluation of learning.

The learners are introduced to the ideas about which method to use and what audio-visual material is appropriate. Hence, the emphasis is not upon training but, instead, is based upon providing insight into the pedagogical processes with imitation and drill discouraged. Training, where appropriate, is founded upon the basic programme. Additionally, the teacher is not expected to come to terms with abstract theory at such a level that it bears no relationship to the reality of daily practice. Instead it is hoped that by relating the theory to practice a much greater transfer between the two can occur.

THE MODEL OF THE BERUFSFORDERUNGS INSTITUTE

An innovative theory of emancipatory learning in occupational training, such as that at Lempert, is a necessary prerequisite for employee-orientated training. In this manner, adult education in a democratic state can make a contribution to both the ability of the individual to be self-determining and also the democratisation of society. Occupational adult education especially should assist the individual towards greater professional autonomy. The ability to behave in an autonomous manner at work is a pre-condition of the movement towards securing democracy in the workplace.

It is therefore necessary to recognise that the aims of a course like this include concepts such as: emancipation, democracy, equality, socio-economic relations, sensitive and reflective behaviour, co-operation and solidarity, initiative, improvement in teaching techniques for adult and continuing education.

OTHER INITIATIVES IN THE TRAINING OF ADULT EDUCATORS

In the past few years there have been two other initiatives in the training and further training of teachers of adults. Since 1986, the pedagogic academies, which are responsible for the training of school teachers, have been granted permission by the Ministry of Education to offer additional courses for those who wish to teach adults. The major emphases of these courses include the study of the functions of training and education. It is envisaged that the student shall be familiar with the functions of the adult school and of adult education and that the possible areas in which adults may study should be known and understood. In addition students should be able to put the elements of adult education theory to practical use. Finally, they shall have some knowledge of the aims, methods and programmes of various adult education institutions.

The second initiative concerns a certificate for the preparation of adult educators in which the following areas of study are envisaged: target groups and participants in adult education, teaching and learning objectives in adult education, content of adult education, planning and conducting courses, methods and media, marketing and publicising adult education, evaluation of adult education. These study areas are arranged in the form of projects or other participant-orientated teaching methods in order to demonstrate the most effective approach to teaching adults.

TRAINING COURSE OF THE STANDING CONFERENCE FOR ADULT EDUCATION

The various organisations for adult education have, for many years, organised a four-week seminar for those workers who are not teachers but who are concerned mainly with the organisation and planning of adult education. Such course participants include secretaries and other workers who already have some experience in their work. The subjects covered during these seminars include: pedagogy, communication, organisation and marketing, law and adult education, and general issues relating to adult education. A certificate of attendance is granted at the end of each one of these short courses.

11   Training in the Federal Republic of Germany

Johannes Weinberg

TWO LARGE SECTORS OF ADULT EDUCATION

In the Federal Republic of Germany vocational education, as well as general adult education, is part of educational politics. Nevertheless, job-orientated training and re-training are both usually carried out by industrial and commercial institutions. Thus there are at least two large sectors of adult education. One is the outcome of the legislation of the federal states (*Länder*), and the other is the outcome of the needs of industry and commerce.

To understand the role of the federal states it is necessary to recognise that they are responsible for cultural and school affairs. During the 1970s most of them passed adult education laws, the purpose of which has been to ensure that the local adult education centres (*Volkshochschulen*) (VHS) and other independent adult education institutions organise courses. This means that besides the local education authorities with their own adult education centres, the churches, trade unions, sports associations, political parties and many other organisations have developed their own adult education provision and are, therefore, part of the adult education system of the Federal Republic. In fact, it is not really a system but a pluralist structure of institutions trying to serve the needs of the adult population.

PUBLIC RESPONSIBILITY

Although the governments of the federal states are not obliged to organise adult education programmes parallel to the school system, they have always felt responsible for the support of the respective adult education institutions. This stems from the constitution of the Weimar Republic (1918-33) which states, 'the popular education (*Volksbildungswesen*), including the folk high schools (*Volkshochschulen*), shall be improved by the National

Government, the Federal Government and the Local Authorities' (para 148.4). After the defeat of the Nazi regime in 1945 quite a number of constitutions of the federal states assumed this tradition. Moreover, in 1947 the convention of municipal authorities had recommended the improvement of adult education and out-of-school youth education to the municipal authorities.

During the 1960s it was the German Folk High School Association (*Deutscher Volkshochschulverband*)[1] which first discussed the question of full-time staff in the public sector. In the late 1960s most of the national adult education associations agreed that to have full-time staff would be of some help. Nevertheless, from the beginning of this period it had always been emphasised that the part-time teachers in adult education should never be fully replaced by full-time personnel.

PLANNING COMMITTEES AND LEGISLATION

In the Federal Republic of Germany in the 1960s and early 1970s, called the years of political innovation of the educational system (*Bildungsreform-Politik*), a number of planning committees were established on both a federal and a national level. Their task was to outline the future structure of pre-school, school, university and post-school education. As far as adult education was concerned, the aim was to develop a new sector of the educational system called 'continuing education' (*Weiterbildung*) instead of adult education (*Erwachsenenbildung*). This former term was defined by the German Educational Council as 'the continuation or resumption of organised learning after the completion of an initial educational phase of varying length'. Continuing education, as it is emphasised, relates to all areas of life.

In all the plans being published during that time, special attention was drawn to the question of full-time and part-time adult educators, especially in the state of North-Rhine Westphalia, where the planning committee for adult and continuing education specified the tasks of full-time adult education personnel.

Although the adult education sector was designated to become an integrated part of the educational system as a whole, the pluralistic range of institutions had to be taken into consideration. The independent status of the particular institutions had to be maintained, so that special attention was given to the following three principles: the right to decide on the educational provision should lie in the hands of each institution; the courses and classes must be open to everybody; the individual must have the right to choose which courses he/she wishes to attend. Taking these principles into account it is clear that full-time adult educators are doing their work outside the framework of school regulations as we know them from the general and vocational school system. Working in an adult education institution means developing and managing our own framework so as to produce courses adequate to the needs of adults. Therefore the planning commission of North-Rhine Westphalia stressed the fact that the most important task of the educational personnel (*pädagogisches Weiterbildungspersonal*) is to manage and plan the educational provision, including rooms, finances, etc.

In practical terms the planning commission asked for full-time principals to be running the institutions and full-time staff (*pädagogische Mitarbeiter*) to develop courses and classes. As an outcome of these recommendations the need for full-time personnel was put into the adult education legislation of North-Rhine Westphalia, including regulations as to how to finance and give status to this new type of pedagogue. Moreover, in all the adult education acts at a state level, it has been laid down that, at least for the administration of an acknowledged adult education institution, a full-time principal should be appointed.

Yet the planning commission did not only consider managing the institution and planning the programme, it also stressed the importance of having good teachers and tutors (*Kursleiter, Dozenten*) to undertake the direct work in the courses. In order to describe the special meaning of teaching in adult education the planning commission introduced a new term, micro-didactical work, (*mikro-didaktische Tatigkeiten*) whilst others preferred the term 'teacher of adults' (*Weiterbildungslehrer*). The idea of the planning commission was to make clear that teaching adults, and adult learning, differ from teaching boys and girls in the classroom. By employing the new term, micro-didactical work, two aspects were being emphasised as being typical of adult education: direct communication in small groups, or at least discussion of a special topic or subject.

Subsequently another term was introduced into the adult education legislation which also describes the field of direct communication between tutor and learners. This term is organised learning (*organisiertes Lernen*). Up to the present time it has been very important in being regarded as a term the administration has been able to understand. Organised learning is not just classroom teaching; it also has a different meaning

131

from both counselling and therapy. Putting this in a more positive way, one might say that organised learning consists of three elements: a topic, an aim and continuing tutor-learner communication.

To conclude this historical introduction, it may be seen that in all the planning papers in the 1960s and early 1970s there is an emphasis upon the improvement of both managing and planning adult education, as well as upon teaching. Those who were demanding full-time staff laid stress upon strengthening the adult education institutions. Thus in the first place full-time personnel were employed for managing and planning purposes.

IMPROVING ADULT EDUCATION BY IMPROVING THE PERSONNEL

It was the institutions and the independent adult education associations, not the universities and teacher training colleges, which began to ask for better qualified personnel. They were looking for experts, men and women, having both the appropriate knowledge and the ability to transmit this to others. As early as the 1920s, it was clear that two relevant questions were already being asked: *what* to teach and *how* to teach it. The former question meant asking for the specialist aspects of the subject, i.e. didactics, while the latter asked for the identification of the appropriate means to teach it, i.e. pedagogy.

During the 1960s a third question was added: what do adults *expect* and for what *purpose* do they wish to learn it? As I understand it, this third question was the real beginning of adult education in the Federal Republic of Germany. This way of questioning was influenced by American, British, Canadian and Swedish outcomes of social research and it was continued by German scholars. When having perceived that adults are not primarily interested in the subject itself, but in the subject as part of their own lives and purposes, the philosophy of adult education had found a firm ground.

This story might be typically German, but it is part of our history since Kurt Lewin, for example, was one of those who had been forced to leave our country and subsequently undertook research relevant to adult education in his adopted country, the United States of America. Additionally, it took time to transmit the outcomes of the social sciences from the western world to the field of adult education in West Germany.

Returning to the 1960s, it is important to note that during this decade the questions of qualified adult education personnel were discussed with reference to the social sciences: psychology, social psychology and sociology began to influence those seeking to improve the work of adult educators and asking how they could gain qualification. Two types of activity began to emerge at the end of the 1950s and the beginning of the 1960s: short meetings and weekend courses for the re-training of part-time adult educators; longer-term courses of four weeks for the preparation of those who intended to work full-time in the field. The first type of course has increased in number annually and at the present time each adult education association and all types of adult education institution offer their own re-training programmes. The second type of course was run by the adult education associations until the end of the 1970s but, since that time, a shortage of finance has meant that no new jobs have been created and, consequently, these courses have ceased to exist.

Both forms of provision were developed by the adult education institutions themselves. During the 1970s, when professoriates of adult education were established in a number of universities and teacher universities a new type of training scheme was established. This new type of course leads to a Diploma in Pedagogics (*Diplom-Pädagogik*) and lasts for four years. During the final two years of the course the student can choose specialist options, such as: pre-school education, social education, adult education. This course of study can now be taken at any of twenty-seven universities in the Federal Republic of Germany.

It has often been asked whether those who have studied adult education as a specialist field would have good career prospects. In general the answer would be in the affirmative. Before the cuts in the public budget, educationalists with this diploma had opportunities to obtain full-time employment. In 1977, out of the 1,603 educationalists having this qualification 220 (13.7 per cent) were working full-time in adult education. From a study in 1979 asking for the statistics of full-time adult educators at local adult education centres (*Volkshochschulen*) 146 (12.5 per cent) out of a total of 1,171 full-timers held this diploma. These figures demonstrate that a small proportion of full-time staff have already gained this qualification. From a similar study in 1978 examining the whole field of adult education 8.6 per cent of full-time adult educators held the Diploma in Pedagogics with a special qualification in adult education. Indeed, it can be seen that about 9.5 per cent of all adult educators held this qualification at the end of the 1970s.

This is important because most of the adult education institutions are likely to reject those who have studied adult education, preferring staff who have passed their examinations in a subject or discipline that could be taught within the institution. But those concentrating on the traditional disciplines ignore the fact that pedagogues of the new type do know quite a lot about socialisation, communication in small groups, family and out-of-school education, etc. Currently these topics are playing an important role in adult education as well as the traditional subject areas. Nevertheless, it should not be forgotten that the representatives of the adult education field have good reasons to insist upon what they have claimed from the outset, i.e. the need for full-time personnel to have passed the university examinations. However, we need not only educationalists but specialists from the technical areas and the humanities.

The main reason for arguing this way has been that full-time adult educators responsible for planning courses must be able to communicate with part-time staff representing the whole range of professional knowledge and experience and this means that adult education institutions need a full team representing all the different subject areas and fields of practical experience. Hence, it seems reasonable to have one, or perhaps two, educationalists of the new type in a team of five, or perhaps ten, full-timers. But it is also sensible not to recruit only pedagogues, as the figures above seem to indicate.

Although there is no need for so many adult educators to hold the Diploma in Pedagogics, there is an increasing need for more knowledge of managing adult education institutions, programme planning and course teaching. The reason for these increasing needs may be that adult education is still an expanding field of activity, with an increasing number of part-time teachers and volunteers. For example, the folk high schools had, in 1984, 117,607 men and women working as part-time teachers and in 1985 this figure was 122,206, a growth of 3.9 per cent. The long-term development can be shown by looking at the statistics ten years ago, when there were only 81,279 in 1977. Because statistics are incomplete no overall figure can be given but the folk high schools do, at least, indicate the trend that is occurring in adult education generally.

To meet the demand for more and better knowledge useful to those working in adult education a new type of short-term study course has been developed in the last few years. These study courses are different from the short re-training activities (*Mitarbeiterfortbildung*) mentioned above. They are primarily organised to exchange experiences and to gain new insights and new knowledge by so doing. In contrast these new study courses do try to transmit a body of knowledge and theory arising from research.

The target groups of such short-term study courses, more or less at university level, are the newcomers to the field and also those who have already been working in the field for some time. Some of these study courses are on their way to becoming acknowledged syllabuses at universities. Most of them consist of a core of printed material for self-study, although direct teaching is not excluded.

The origin and emerging processes of these study courses differ very much from each other. Nevertheless, all have one element in common — they are the outcome of close co-operation between university people and personnel from the institutions and associations of adult education.

Short descriptions of some of these study courses are given below: three of them have already been published by the European Bureau of Adult Education in its Geiranger Report (1982).

RESEARCH-BASED KNOWLEDGE FOR ADULT EDUCATORS

These short study-courses are aimed at full-time and part-time personnel in adult education and aim to serve their needs in the areas of research-based knowledge. Alternatively, by developing, realising and implementing these courses university staff have tried to open the 'ivory tower' to adult educators in the field. They also hope to learn from the people in the field about what they expect from the universities. Both sides are interested in learning by doing things together. On the side of the university staff the assumption is that this co-operation is not merely a process of disseminating knowledge, but it could be a process of transforming knowledge into experience and from experience into new knowledge.

The following descriptions show that the short study-courses are offered by particular adult education associations, while others are offered by university staff or even by departments.

1. The self-study materials (*Selbstudienmaterial*): These were developed by the Pedagogical Institute of the German Folk High School Association (*Pädagogische Arbeitsstelle des Deutschen Volkshochschulverbandes*) in close association with a number of adult educators and university staff. Twenty-four study units (*Studieneienheiten*) cover four subject areas:

- social background and conditions of adult education,
- institutional and organisational problems of the folk high schools,
- programme planning and course-work preparation in adult education,
- the process of learning and teaching in adult education.

2. Materials to qualify part-time adult educators (*NQ-Materialien*): These were developed and edited by a working group from university adult education (*Arbeitskreis Universität Erwachsenenbildung* — AUE) in co-operation with the University of Oldenburg. The eight learning units cover one main area only: teaching and learning with adults, mainly aspects of communication and motivation.

3. The course system of the University of Distance Studies in Hagen (*das Studiensystem der Fernuniversität in Hagen*). This has been developed by the university in co-operation with quite a number of university personnel throughout the Federal Republic and also in close contact with the adult education associations, including those which represent trade and commerce. The package of more than twenty units covers the same subject areas as the self-study materials developed with the Folk High School Association, together with the history of adult education and teaching methods for particular subjects, e.g. languages.

4. Teaching and Learning a Foreign Language (*Erwachsenengemasses Lehren und Lernen einer Fremdsprache — Sprachandragogik*). This has been developed by the Extra-Mural Department of the University of Mainz in co-operation with the Seminar for English, the Seminar for Romanic Languages, and representatives of the folk high schools in the vicinity of Mainz. The syllabus covers six subject areas:

- analysing textbooks and curriculum planning,
- media for foreign-language teaching and how to use them in the classroom,
- counselling,
- methods and forms of teaching and learning,
- methods of evaluation and examination adequate for adults,
- realising classroom teaching.

The syllabus consists of a number of small learning units, from which the students can select those in which they are interested. If they seek a certificate, then they must accumulate a given number of learning units in each subject area and write a thesis (*Hausarbeit*) and undergo a colloquium (*Prüfungscolloquium*) at the end.

The course is recognised as a refresher course (*Kontakstudium*) by the University of Mainz, so that access is restricted to those who already hold university entrance qualifications (the *Abitur*), have good language competence and have some experience in language teaching.

5. Protestant Institute for Distance Studies for Volunteers and Employees of the Church (*Evangelische Arbeitsstelle Fernstudium für kirkchliche Dienste* in Hannover): This is part of an extensive syllabus, including special topics on theology and the religious life. The basic course (*Grundkurs*) related to adult education in general consists of five lessons in the form of self-study materials:

- theory of Protestant adult education,
- learning and fields of learning for adults,
- didactics (*didaktisches Handeln*),
- methods of adult education,
- understanding group processes and working with groups.

In addition, materials have also been developed covering special fields, such as parent and family education (*Eltern- und Familienbildung*), learning with elderly people (*Altenbildung*) and religion in everyday life (*Glaube im Alltag*).

The project began in 1970 and currently the materials are being revised. The aim is to have the self-study materials starting from the experience of the learner. Although great emphasis is placed upon the materials, social learning (*Lernen in Gruppen*) is also an integrated part of the course. During the last years the institute has developed a network of study circles (*Studienzirkel*) and block-seminars (*Blockseminare*) to enable mutual counselling and practical exercises.

These examples may give an impression of the study courses having been developed over the past few years. But at the moment there is no publication which provides an overall picture of all the courses although some more detailed information may be found in the periodical *Literatur und Forschungs Report Weiterbildung* (17), (Seibert and Weinburg).

PROBLEMS AND FUTURE NEEDS

The first steps during the 1970s to make public adult education a part of the educational system were stopped at the beginning of the 1980s. Nevertheless adult education, including further education and adult vocational training, is a growing field. Those working in it, volunteers, part-timers and full-timers are becoming aware that they need special training and re-training. The adult education institutions are asking for full-time personnel, not only for managing and programme planning, but also for teaching and counselling. There is also a need for full-time specialists in the field of the new 'media' for learning.

Whatever the status and the income of adult educators, they consider that adults expect an increasing number of learning opportunities for the purposes of gaining qualifications. Therefore, the re-training of those already working in the field and the preparation and introduction of those who want to enter it is very important. This should be done by combining research findings and everyday experiences. And by so doing, it is important to add that training and trainers should no longer be just an episode. I would like to insist and say re-training should be a continuous process. There is no reason why an airline pilot should have to undergo a check on his skills every year but that an adult educator should need no more than commonsense thinking and doing.

As I understand it, the requirements that adult education has to tackle include the need for research based on knowledge and skills to enable adult educators to stimulate two-way learning processes. We need more learning teachers and teaching learners than we have at the moment. Following this line of reasoning means that we need open access to all opportunities, including universities, so that people working in adult education can refresh their knowledge and skills. This also means that we need more research in all the subject areas already included in the courses mentioned above, preferably in the field of management and programme planning, classroom teaching, group work, intercultural learning and women's education. There seems to be a lack of systematic research and knowledge in these areas. Most of the remarks offered here, which are true for public sector adult education, are also true for adult education in industry and commerce.

NOTE

1. Address: Rheinallee 1, D-5300 Bonn 2, Federal Republic of Germany.

BIBLIOGRAPHY

Adult Education in the Federal Republic of Germany (1985) Bonn: Secretariat of the Standing Conference of the Ministers of Education and Cultural Affairs of the Länder of the Federal Republic of Germany.

Dolff, H. (1979) 'West German experience of popular higher education', in Schuller, T. and Megarry, J. (eds) *World Yearbook on Education*, London: Kogan Page.

Pfluger, A. (1980) '*Zur beruflichen Situation der Diplomadagogen/Erwachsenen-bildung im Volkshochschulbereich – Ergebnisse einer DVV-Umfrage'*, *Materialien zur Studien – und Berufssitutation in der Erwachsenenbildung*, no 24, Hannover: Arbeitskreis Universität Erwachsenenbildung.

Siebert, H. and Weinberg, J. (eds) (1986) *Literatur und Forschungs Report Weiterbildung*, Heft 17 Juli, Munster.

Schuller, T. and Megarry, J. (eds) (1979) *World Yearbook on Education*, London: Kogan Page.

Studienmöglichkeiten der Erwachsenenpädogogik an den Hochschulen der Bundersrepublik Deutschland und West Berlins. Materialien zur Studien und Berufssituation in der Erwachsenenbildung, no 31, Hannover: Arbeitskreis Universität Erwachsenenbilding.

Survey of Adult Education Legislation, (1985) Amersfoort: European Bureau of Adult Education.

Training and Further Training of Adult Educators (1982) (Geiranger Report) Amersfoort: European Bureau of Adult Education.

12 Training adult educators in Switzerland

Carl Rohrer

Training in the field of adult education as a whole is offered in Switzerland by four different providers:

1 The University of Geneva offers adult education as a field of specialisation within a faculty degree (licentiate) programme.
2 The Academy for Adult Education in Lucerne offers a part-time course on one afternoon per week, together with residential elements, over three years.
3 The Swiss Federation for Adult Education offers a cycle of six-week residential programmes spread over a three-year period.
4 The Education Department of the Canton of Berne offers a cycle of four one-week residential programmes, combined with supervision in the workplace.

The last of these four has only recently been established and, therefore, this overview will concentrate on the other three organisations.

THE TRAINING OF ADULT EDUCATORS IN THE FACULTIES OF PSYCHOLOGY AND EDUCATION AT THE UNIVERSITY OF GENEVA

The Department of Education consists of five sub-divisions, one of which is designated Adult Education. In this programme the first cycle, or phase, of studies offers a choice of fifteen courses in three basic fields, i.e. introduction to the study of education, study of educational processes and the study of educational systems. The second cycle involves specialisation in one of the five sub-divisions. These focus upon the development and planning of educational systems, didactics and educational practice, adult education, special education and, finally, theory and practice of school education. With regard to Adult Education the curriculum includes two credit units, i.e. courses or seminars, from the basic fields, and eight credit units chosen from among those offered in the sub-division. Finally, one unit forms the preparatory seminar centred on a dissertation or *memoire de licence.* The level of the award of licentiate can be described as being at approximately post-first degree level.

Students of adult education can select from fifteen courses or seminars. Five of them deal with rather general topics such as evaluation, philosophy of education, leading learning groups. Others are more specialised, such as education and mass media. In addition, other themes are especially geared to the needs of people active in certain areas of adult education, such as worker education, continuing education for nurses and literacy work.

One prerequisite of the award is a measure of practical teaching experience. For a minority of students coming directly from upper secondary school it is necessary to undertake teaching for a certain length of time but the majority of students have already fulfilled this requirement having been teachers for many years.

In all five sub-divisions of the Education Department a special certificate of continuing education is offered to graduates of any university department who have worked in a profession for at least three years. This certificate can be obtained by full-time study of at least two semesters and by the completion of at least two basic and seven specialised credit units. Practitioners, such as trainers from industry and commerce, or tutors of evening classes for adults comprise approximately 10 per cent of the student body of the Adult Education sub-division.

With regard to action research projects, the adult education sub-division is closely involved in providing special courses for trainers involved in such areas of work as patient education and programmes for unemployed adults.

The University of Geneva is the only Swiss university which, in certain faculties, admits students who have not obtained a *baccalaureate,* i.e. school completion diploma award, which gives the holder the right to enter the appropriate field of study for a higher qualification. The university's candidates follow an individualised admission scheme which, above all, takes into account life experience and the professional projects which have been undertaken.

In the last decade many graduates in education, specialising in adult education, have been trained at the University of Geneva.

THE ACADEMY FOR ADULT EDUCATION IN LUCERNE

The Academy for Adult Education was founded in 1971 at a time when the education of adults was regarded as a new field of practice and the adult educator as a new type of professional facing many and varied challenges inside and outside the institutional framework, which includes vocational training and updating. The stated aim of the academy is to spread and promote adult education. The politically independent organisation, also free of church domination, is controlled in all matters relating to administration, finance and educational policies by a supervisory board; it is subsidised by the canton and city of Lucerne as well as by the national government.

Three courses are offered. The first leads to a Diploma in Adult Education and is aimed at part-time tutors. The second is concerned with the full-time professionals and concentrates on the training of trainers. The third one focuses upon youth and community work. This section concentrates upon the part-time diploma rather than the other two. However, the significance of the training of the trainers is something to which further reference is made elsewhere in this volume.

The diploma course in adult education involves attendance on ninety afternoons spread over a three-year period and, in addition, there are twenty-seven days of residential weeks and weekends during the same period. Tutorials, intensive reading and the completion of assignments require another three to seven hours each week.

The underlying aim of the course emphasises practical teaching and its relationship to the theoretical aspects of adult education. The process of learning is a shared experience of course participants and course tutors. The former are encouraged to help influence and shape the course content, its organisation and the choice of the methods employed. Constant appraisal and evaluation is considered an essential part of the learning process, while personal and professional experiences are regarded as being valuable resources for all involved in the course.

Course participants are adult education tutors who, having gained a professional qualification in their own subject area as well as relevant work experience, now feel committed to their teaching. Open-mindedness, a willingness to accept new ideas, self discipline and sheer stamina are considered essential attributes. Anyone simply wishing to find another way of earning a living, or seeking a way out of a personal crisis by attending a study programme are considered to be unsuitable candidates for this course of study.

The content covers four main areas:

- The adult learner as an individual, interpersonal relations between learners and the adult learners' position in Swiss society.
- Group dynamics and interaction, facilitation of learning, barriers to adults learning.
- The learning environment, adult learning in the socio-cultural context.
- Methods and approaches used in the facilitation of learning.

Practical teaching in the classroom is supervised by a support tutor during the whole of the three-year period, but subject specialism is unnecessary as it does not constitute part of the course.

In order to gain the diploma, the candidates are required to attend regularly and to submit a lengthy report which must be their own reflections on their own teaching experiences and upon the wider aspects of the theory and practice of adult education. A formal interview completes the assessment process.

THE SWISS FEDERATION FOR ADULT EDUCATION (SFAE)

Shortly after establishing a permanent secretariat in 1966, the SFAE, the umbrella organisation of private non-profit making providers, was invited by its members to develop a training scheme for adult educators. Part-time teachers and group leaders were identified as forming the main target group. In order to attract sufficient numbers the target area was extended to encompass the whole of German-speaking Switzerland. It was decided that the training scheme format should be composed of five-day residential blocks. This proved to be useful as a means of fostering informal sharing of experiences between adult educators of different status working in different fields.

The first pilot course was offered in 1969 and, thereafter, the planned course cycle consisting of four weeks training spread over two years commenced in 1970. A fifth week, focused on project work as a means of summarising and applying learning achieved on the courses, was offered as optional in 1975 and that part was made compulsory in 1982 in order to gain the SFAE course cycle participation certificate. In 1984, a sixth week concerning growth of and development in organisations was added to the compulsory cycle.

The fifth week's programme, by the nature of its theme,

requires participation in the preceding four weeks; otherwise the weeks are considered as independent modules that can be taken in any chosen order. As a new cycle commences every two years a week missed due to professional or private reasons may be taken two years later in order to complete the cycle. Minimum completion time is approximately two and a half years.

The content and objectives of the six weeks are outlined below:

Week 1: Adult Teaching and Learning Techniques: Different teaching and learning techniques — group discussion, buzz groups, lectures, etc. — are demonstrated and then practised by participants. They are encouraged to reflect on, re-evaluate and present their subject matter in accordance with the interests of their students. Through engaging in small-group project work participants have the opportunity to experience enjoyable and meaningful learning.

Week 2: Design and Use of Teaching Aids and Other Visual Media: Participants produce software and also handle aids such as overhead projectors, felt boards and charts. They learn about graphic design and reproduction techniques for prospectuses, worksheets, etc. In considering and using a variety of teaching aids participants will have their own subjects in mind; they will be assisted individually and in small project groups by specialists who, in part, are drawn from commercial companies dealing in teaching technology or photography. A major focus is placed on the plenary sessions during and at the end of the block when projects are demonstrated and commented upon.

Week 3: Communication and Co-operation in Adult Education: During this week participants learn more about how they relate to each other and how they can co-operate. They consider ways of transferring their experiences to their own teaching and/or organisational situation. Greater conceptual changes have taken place in this particular week resulting from a developing sense of emancipation brought about through the practice of group dynamics and towards a design in which self-awareness exercises are seen not as ends in themselves but as being embedded in reflections upon the learning goals.

Week 4: General Didactics and Evaluation in Adult Education: The participants assess curricular determinants, describe learning objectives and plan different phases of teaching units and courses. They apply this knowledge to planning or revising their own courses. This workshop phase is enriched by inputs about methodological and motivational elements. Finally, an exhibition of courses, diagrams elaborated upon by individuals or groups, and the presentation of sample lessons allow for discussion about the solutions to the problems chosen. One topic of the week is the identification and evaluation of learning progress.

Week 5: Developing Course Programmes: In this phase of the cycle the intentions of the trainers are aimed less at the whole group than at individual participants who offer a practical planning task drawn from their particular field of activity. This services as a basis for the repetition, deepening and application of the content of the four weeks of basic preparation. Here again, mutual preparation and appraisal of projects helps to improve didactic and methodological expertise of course members.

Week 6: Adult Educators in Organisations: Structural barriers and tensions between different groups of personnel may reduce the efficiency of the services offered. This cycle commences with the working situation of the participants who are invited to analyse their organisations, plan changes and foster development processes, thereby becoming more aware of existing forms of dependency. The general information leaflet for this particular phase identifies people working in the field of adult education and, thereby, having some group work experience, as the primary target for attention. The course therefore provides a means of clarifying and solving problems already experienced by group members.

Although the course may be considered as initial training with respect to organised teaching, it is — or should be — continuing education with respect to the whole of the participants' experience in adult education. Only by building upon this background experience can the course be so short in duration. This explanation has proved to be necessary as a certain percentage of the applicants tend to mistake the SFAE course as a means of entering the field of adult education for the first time. This is in contrast to traditional professional training whereby completion ensures that successful trainees are eligible for certain posts.

In comparison to this traditional model, the SFAE course, and some other training opportunities for adult educators in Switzerland, present typical features of a recurrent model of preparation for professional and voluntary roles. Therefore, a report from Switzerland to the Organisation for Economic Co-operation and Development (OECD 1975) included this course cycle in a number of case studies of recurrent education in this country.

Participants working for SFAE member organisations benefit from reduced fees and registration priority, but the course is open to all who have or foresee some opportunity to apply the knowledge and skills acquired. It has usually been possible to admit those remaining on the waiting list and on the few occasions when it has not been practicable a course week has had to be repeated.

A limiting factor is language. The Swiss-German dialect is associated with informality and intimacy by its speakers, while High German is associated with formality; thus, the course has been held in the dialect. French-speaking and Italian-speaking Swiss colleagues and Germans and Austrians from neighbouring regions must be able to understand the dialect if they are to participate.

NOTE

The Editors wish to thank Mrs E. Arthur from Goldsmiths College, University of London, who provided some of the information about the Academy of Adult Education in Lucerne.

BIBLIOGRAPHY

Bottani, Norbert *et al.* (1975) *Rekurrente Bildung in der Scweiz. Entwicklungstendenzen und Perspekitven. Bericht der Schweiz an das Zentrum für Bildungsforschung (CERI) in der OECD*, Paris: OECD (Wissen-schaftspolitik, Berheft) pp. 29ff.

Claude, A. (1974) *Ausbildung von Erwachsenenbildern in der Schweiz. In Erwachsenenbildung* (ed KBE Bonn), vol 20, no 1 pp. 25ff.

Claude, A. (1977) *Zur Institutionalisierung der Aus- und Fortbildung von Erwachsenenbildern in der Schweiz. In Qualifizierung des Weiterbildungspersonals in Oesterreich und in der Schweiz*, Hannover: Arbeitskreis Universitäre Erwachsenenbildung/AUE (MAEB, Heft 9) pp. 22 ff.

Part V

Scandinavian countries

13 The supplementary training of teachers in voluntary adult education in Denmark

Ivan Häuser

In Denmark adult and youth education is subject to a major law, the Voluntary Education Act of 1968. In the introduction to this chapter some of its main features are noted and, also, some of its weaknesses. The first section then describes the complex system of adult education in this country. The second section, concerning the preparation of adult educators, also opens with reference to this Act and then goes on to discuss their training.

The idea behind the Voluntary Education Act of 1968 was that people should be able to meet freely to discuss questions of common interest, and that this then furthers the democratic processes of society. The requirements for establishing adult education courses are very liberal: if a minimum of twelve people wish to be taught a certain subject, the course must be offered and the central government and the municipality must cover two-thirds of the teachers' fees and administration costs, while the participants cover the remaining third. There are very few fields in which classes cannot be set up under the Voluntary Education Act — but these do include ballroom dancing, jazz, ballet and bridge. Anybody who has participated in a forty-eight hour teachers' course is entitled to establish such courses under the Voluntary Education Act (Act on Leisure Time Education — *Lov om Fritidsundervisning*). This has resulted in the existence of about 3,000 evening schools in Denmark today, some being very small with up to five classes, whilst others are much larger. The small and medium-sized schools invariably have their administrative offices in the private residence of the head of the school whilst the largest sixty-eight schools have their offices in the town centre and employ between five and thirty office workers. Handicapped people are entitled to an equal chance of participating in popular education activities and this participation is made more possible by the provision of favourable terms and an allowance is made for the handicap: in handicapped persons' groups there has only to be a minimum of five persons, as opposed to twelve, and these activities are entirely free. In addition, classes for immigrants used to be covered by this special education legislation, but now there are separate regulations.

Among the other provisions of the Act is concern for teacher training for this group of teachers. Indeed, the associations are granted funds in order to conduct these courses and teachers are expected to have some form of qualification. It will be to this part of the Act that the second section of this chapter turns its attention.

There are some weaknesses in the Act, as we are presently discovering, some of which are mentioned below. As already stated, there are many people in Denmark who undertake voluntary leisure-time education but, as the term implies, it is meant for education in the leisure time. Today approximately half the classes take place in the daytime and most of the daytime participants are unemployed or retired people all of whose time might be viewed as leisure time. This gives rise to problems of accommodation. Most of the publicly owned premises, such as *Folkeskoler*, are fully occupied then. For many unemployed, in particular, voluntary education has become a way of life, at least from 8a.m. to 4p.m. replacing the occupation and fulfilling the need for social activity. However, this is a function that voluntary education simply cannot perform since the participants cannot afford the fees to cover the one-third of the salary costs of the teachers for so many lessons.

In addition, the Danish Voluntary Education Act was formulated at a time when we were much more naïve about equal opportunities. Voluntary educational activities have never really attracted those people who have most need of them and have the most serious social problems, so that there is a need for outreach (*Opsøgende virksomhed*) but these forms of activities are not included within the framework of the Act.

The Act has also maintained the age-group divisions within society for, while children are allowed to attend the same courses as their parents, they have to pay the same fee which makes education a costly affair beyond the reach of many families. Grants are offered, under the terms of the Act, to individual groups for teachers' salaries, but this makes interdisciplinary projects and activities without a teacher difficult. Having examined some of the points regarding this Act it is now important to consider the provision of adult and youth education in Denmark.

ADULT EDUCATION IN GENERAL

Altogether the various forms of adult education in Denmark constitute a rather mixed bag. There is no single educational system, as will be shown below, and a wide variety of developmental and educational opportunities for adults exist. The following pages seek to record some of these opportunities in a systematic manner.

Adult Danes can choose between various academic-orientated or labour market-orientated education, ranging from courses that lead to qualifying examinations (at *Folkeskoler* or *Gymnasium*) to workshop-like courses designed to give participants an idea of both job and educational opportunities, e.g. vocationally orientated courses in schools for semi-skilled workers. In addition, public and private organisations offer extensive internal educational opportunity where employees/members can update their knowledge and skills, be re-trained or merely enjoy personal development. Such activity may take place in a study centre of a company or organisation, but often businesses pay for the employee to participate in a voluntary leisure-time educational activity or in specialised studies at a business or commercial school. In Denmark, those activities that are aimed mainly at personal development and those in popular, youth and adult education which are designed for participation in the democratic processes of the country are collectively known as general education. However, there is no clear-cut dividing line between it and vocationally orientated education. At folk high schools, for example, it is possible to take a qualifying examination such as an agricultural certificate, i.e. a Green Certificate, that qualifies the holder to run a farm. Additionally, some evening schools run courses which prepare students to sit for examinations. While it is not possible to draw this distinction clearly, since it is not possible to separate a person's working life from that of being a member of society, it should be mentioned that there are major differences between the Danish tradition in adult and youth education on the one hand and vocational education on the other.

The following paragraphs outline some of the different providers of education for adults in Denmark; they occur in no order of preference or hierarchy. They are presented in this way only to show the reader the complexity of provision for adult education in our country.

Evening schools (*aftenskoler*)

The most comprehensive adult education activity in Denmark, measured in terms of the number of participants, is voluntary or leisure-time education. About one-fifth of all Danes participate in voluntary education of some kind, with courses ranging from physical training (e.g. yoga, physical exercise, relaxation) to creative subjects (e.g. sewing, handicrafts, music) and to languages, etc.

In many cases the evening schools are established by political adult education associations, e.g. the Workers' Educational Association (AOF) which is itself affiliated to the workers' movement and to the Social Democratic Party and the Popular Educational Association which is connected with the Conservative Party; or they have a more or less definite political association, e.g. The Free Educational Association (FO) which is liberal; or they have attachments to popular movements in the grass roots, e.g. Critical Educational Association; or they are related to some of the other wider associations — housewives' associations, sports associations. In contrast, other evening schools emphasise their independence and do not wish to be associated with any particular philosophy; this is the official policy of those who have joined together in the national association known as the Danish Adult Educational Association (DOF). In fact, most evening schools seem to have a wide appeal regardless of their ideological point of departure, with neither the teachers not the participants being easily placed in categories, either socially or politically. This certainly reflects the position in recent years as the Danish population has moved in different directions, with some of the new groupings still being difficult to identify. Hence, some evening schools are characterised by great diversity and offer courses in almost every conceivable subject — the most popular ones being:

- Physical education, with 18 per cent of all participants.
- Music, with 12 per cent.
- Handicrafts, e.g. weaving, painting, textiles, drawing, ceramics, etc., with 12 per cent.
- Dress-making, cutting out, with 10 per cent.
- Foreign-language (English, German, French, Spanish), with 10 per cent.
- Cooking, domestic science, with 6 per cent.
- EDP, with 2 per cent.

Classes take place mainly in premises, e.g. *Folkeskole*, which are empty in the afternoon and in these instances, *Folkeskole* facilities, such as video equipment and overhead projectors, must be placed at the disposal of evening schools. However, there are grants and subsidies available towards the rent of private premises, which the evening schools might require for their frequent daytime classes.

Youth schools (*Ungdomsskoler*)

There is a tradition in Denmark that voluntary youth education, which takes place in the so-called youth schools, is considered as adult education and it is, therefore, subject to the Voluntary Education Act. About 60 per cent of all young people (fourteen to eighteen years old) participate in one or more classes in the youth school; they may also meet in the youth school club and may attend, for instance, classes in creative subjects or participate in survival courses. Classes in youth schools are free, with central government paying municipalities a general subsidy and it is the latter which both finances and approves the youth schools. It is actually possible for young people who wish to leave the *Folkeskole* to spend the final part of their compulsory schooling in a youth school. In these instances they spend the whole day at youth school. Here there is no compulsory curriculum and so it is possible to adapt the classes to the interests of the pupils. Youth schools are frequently located as annexes, or in some cases as part of, the local *Folkeskole*. In all cases, however, the youth schools have rooms of their own and, in some instances, they actually have separate buildings.

Youth clubs (*Ungdomsklubber*)

Besides the youth school clubs, which are only open to youth school pupils, there are other clubs for young people which usually cater for those who do not belong to any organisation or club, e.g. sports clubs and political associations, and who have difficulty in keeping themselves occupied and are, consequently, at risk of becoming engaged in criminal activities. These clubs are administered by the local welfare and health authorities.

Folk high schools (*Folkehøjskoler*)

In these schools students live in residence and the schools themselves are state-subsidised, according to the number of groups/courses which they can establish. Like the evening schools, the folk high schools may offer a wide range of courses including languages, theatre, music and handicrafts. In addition, there are specialised folk high schools and those which specialise in running refresher courses for organisations seem to be very successful. However, the more traditional ones seem to be failing a little, which may be because there have been more schools established in recent years than the market can accommodate. There are, at present, 166 folk high schools, twenty-eight specialising in home economics and another thirty-two in agriculture.

Day folk high schools (*Daghøjskoler*)

The above shortcomings in the Voluntary Education Act were mentioned in order to show that it is now a little out of date and some of its failings are being tackled by the creation of new educational institutions such as day folk high schools and activity centres. These have full-time staffs, unlike most of the evening schools, and participants can become remotivated for further education and work.

Continuation schools (*Efterskoler*)

These are schools for young people, which also offer board and lodging in connection with their educational activities. They are alternative schools at which youngsters may complete their final years of compulsory education. Some of these are specialised, e.g. music schools; others are aimed at young people with special problems, such as dyslexia. Many of these schools are successful in what they seek to undertake. This type of school is included here so that readers can compare it with the following forms of educational provision.

Production schools (*Produktionsskoler*)

Production schools, of which there are about sixty in Denmark, are an innovation aimed at young people and are similar to folk high schools for adults. Here, young people work to make products with a view to selling them, which serves an educational purpose. Some production schools have accommodation, one is a boarding school, and some are integrated with the youth schools mentioned earlier.

Rehabilitation (*Revalidering*)

Like the production schools, the rehabilitation institutions, run by the social welfare authorities, pursue educational objectives through the production of goods which are subsequently sold. Here people who have been 'disconnected with society' because of accident or illness have an opportunity to be re-schooled or re-trained.

Pre-vocational courses (*Erhversintroducerende Kurser*)

People who are unemployed can participate in pre-vocational courses which provide an introduction into a variety of practical subjects. The courses are conducted under the auspices of the schools for semi-skilled workers. Since there are a large number of unemployed people a variety of job-creation projects have been established, with different target groups — such as women who wish to start their own business.

Preparatory courses for examinations (*Prøveforberedende Undervisning*)

The preparatory educational activities under the Voluntary Education Act, which meant that adults could take the school-leaving certificates they were unable to obtain as children, has been a great success, so great in fact that in 1978 this type of education was made subject to separate legislation. This opportunity to acquire qualifications which are endorsed by the educational system in general and which open doors to certain kinds of jobs has attracted participants not previously seen in leisure-time education. These courses are known by a variety of names, including: second-chance education (*Forberedelses-kurses*), single-subject courses (*Enkeltfagskurser*). However, they are the same throughout the country and have attracted a female reserve of intelligence who are now well on their way through the educational system or have moved on to the labour market.

In principle, the same courses are offered in the preparatory education phase as in the final years of the *Folkeskole* and the *Gymnasium*. This development, however, tends towards the adult schools, with their own courses, curricula and examinations. In all, there are now about eighty adult education centres in Denmark.

University extension courses (*Folkeuniversitetet*) and Free access universities (*Åbent Universitet*)

In addition to all of these forms of organisation, there are the libraries which send book buses to scarcely populated areas, arrange exhibitions and public lectures, some even having EDP-rooms where visitors can acquaint themselves with modern technology. Clubs and associations (*Foreninger*) play an important part in Danish life, since nearly all Danes are members of several of these. Clubs and associations can apply to local authorities for grants towards the costs of premises and many have acquired their own premises. Nearly all causes or activities imaginable have their own association and these offer educational activities, often under the auspices of the 1968 Act. People who are actively involved in clubs and associations, e.g. board members and leaders, are considered to be folk educators, just like teachers in folk high schools and evening schools.

In recent years there have been many developments in leisure-time pursuits, including the introduction of 'leisure spots' (*Væresteder*) some of which have creative workshops. Some of these leisure spots are houses of culture, where local professional and amateur artists perform. Other experimental projects include the introduction of EDP-rooms and media workshops. Often these are integrated into established evening school, youth school or folk high school activity. These many projects are meant to create a rich cultural environment in local areas and are also aimed at preventing alienation and crime. Project leaders, leaders and staff at leisure spots, are a new type of folk educator and their primary tasks are to initiate, counsel and be generally available in their communities.

New legislation about adult education

As will be seen from the above description the educational provision currently available in Denmark is far wider than that envisaged by the 1968 Act. There are many indications of the rising demand for local activity centres and for projects that cut across social and institutional divisions; these are not necessarily alternatives to the normal leisure-time adult education but are supplementary to it. Therefore, a three-year experimental programme initiated by the Danish parliament and the Ministry of Education is currently running which is aimed at highlighting the needs for revision of the current legislation. The research for this is being gathered by the National Development Centre for Popular and Adult Education which was established in Copenhagen in 1985.

THE SUPPLEMENTARY TRAINING OF TEACHERS IN ADULT EDUCATION

The teacher of a course . . . must by virtue of his education and previous activities have acquired professional qualifications in the subject matter of the course in question as well as the requisite teaching qualification.

Acceptance of a teacher . . . may in each individual case be made conditional on his or her participation in a course of adult educational theory.

Excerpts from section 7 of the Danish Voluntary Education Act, 1968

As was shown in the previous section, many people are actively involved in Danish popular and adult education in a variety of ways. These are the people to whom teacher training and vocational preparation should be aimed. But an interesting paradox emerges!

In Denmark the persons to whom we entrust our youngest children in professional day care, i.e. day nursery teachers, etc. are required to have four years' training in educational theory and psychology. When at the age of six or seven the children are sent to the municipal primary or lower secondary school (*Folkeskole*) they are also taught by persons with four years of training behind them. However, their four-year training period includes many subjects, other than educational theory and psychology, as these teachers naturally have to acquire skills and knowledge in a number of different subjects. When adolescents go to the upper secondary school (*Gymnasium*), or to a commercial or a technical school they meet teachers whose knowledge of educational theory has been reduced to a course of theory and practice of about six months' duration (*paedagogikum*). If we go one step further and

157

consider teachers at universities and similar educational establishments for adults, there are no longer any requirements with regard to the teachers' training in educational theory and practice. It can be concluded that the age of the pupils varies inversely with the requirements of teacher training in educational theory and practice. The younger the pupils the longer the training, and vice versa. Something seems to indicate that there is no such thing as adult education theory.

This very clear tendency may be attributed to the idea that children are in a 'developing' situation and that in order to teach them we consequently need to know something about their development. In this regard adults are 'completed' persons who know what they want and therefore require nothing from the teacher's expertise except their professional, i.e. subject, skills.

Since the 1950s, adult life has become more changeable and we now probably all recognise that adults grow, develop and change throughout their lives, although developmental psychology still retains a much more narrow approach. Consequently, it might be possible to explain the absence of training requirements for teachers of adults by pointing to our failure to respond to these new conditions within society. This might be an explanation — but there could be another as well.

In Denmark we like to claim that 'the people educates itself', i.e. that we learn from each other. It should be immediately possible for a person who has skills in a particular field, or who feels deeply about something, to be able to teach it to his/her fellow citizens. Some people are good at making clothes and others are proficient in languages; some by virtue of their professional insight, e.g. social legislation, purchase and sale of real estate, child rearing, health, may be able to teach others. Musicians might be able to pass on their skills, etc. If teachers of this type of educational activity are required to undergo training in educational theory, the present easy access to becoming a teacher in adult education may become restricted and adult education teachers would soon start their own occupation, start their own union with its closed-shop agreements, etc. Another consideration is the absence of a traditional teacher—pupil relationship within adult education. The participants are supposed to educate themselves and the teachers are only there to help them do so; the teacher him/herself is a participant in the process of education. The absence of a requirement regarding training in adult education theory may therefore be taken as an expression of the importance attached to the principle that 'the people educates itself'.

Irrespective of whether we choose to adhere to any of the

above explanations, it is maintained here that people involved in adult education need training just as much as managers need training in management, etc. It will also be shown below that serious work is being undertaken in several places in Denmark in order to provide adult educators with the necessary qualifications in educational theory and practice.

However, it is now necessary to examine the occupation of educator of adults.

County advisers

They are employed by the state at county level. There are fourteen counties in all, and they have a number of statutory duties including approving teachers' professional and teaching qualifications and acting as advisers to leisure-time teachers and leaders. County advisers may be assisted by educational and teaching consultants who may, on invitation from teachers and leaders, supervise evening schools and study groups and give advice at meetings or by other means. County advisers also have funds available, as a result of the Voluntary Education Act, to assist in the training of evening and youth school teachers and, in the mid-1970s, this activity became so widespread that supplementary training institutes were established.

The teachers and leaders

Leisure-time education leaders have formed both part-time and full-time leader associations. In addition, associations like the youth organisation, Youth Ring (*Ungdomsringen*), and the Boy and Girl Scout movements have their own training centres for their own leaders. Finally, teachers generally maintain some contact with their own place of education, be it an institute of arts and crafts, a needlework teacher training college, an academy of music, a university, etc. They may also subscribe to professional periodicals and are often invited by their organisations to participate in supplementary training.

The adult education associations

The adult education associations, whose evening schools cover the whole of the country, can under the provisions of the 1968 Act be granted the means to employ advisers to stimulate the

159

internal development of the association through experimental projects, courses and conferences. Many of the evening schools are associated with nation-wide adult education associations and pay the association a fee in return for the advisory guidance and support which is offered by these personnel. Under the provisions of the Act, adult education associations may receive financial support to conduct courses of training for their teachers.

Support services for teachers

In all counties there are teachers' libraries with educational facilities and, in addition, there are county centres for teaching materials (*Amtscentraler for Undervisningsmidler*). Here teachers can examine the latest teaching materials and even borrow them for a more detailed examination. In addition, they can borrow materials for use in class, such as books and topic boxes (e.g. a box of everyday African tools), videos and films. The library should be relevant to existing interests and each county centre has staff and educational advisers, who will help visiting teachers to find the right materials. County centres also conduct study activities aimed at helping to inform the teachers about the use of new materials — they also run short courses (three to five lessons) free of charge.

There is also a National Centre for Teaching Materials (*Landscentralen for Undervisningsmidler*) and it works in conjunction with the county centres. They tape relevant Danish radio and television programmes suitable for educational purposes and then lend them to teachers. Moreover, Danish Radio has a special education department and all the programmes can be borrowed by the county centres from this central department. The national centre also assists the county centres in purchasing foreign video productions and prepares its own in Danish. These centres seek to assist the whole of the world of education in Denmark, but thus far their main clientele appears to have been teachers from the *Folkeskoler*. Gradually their service to adult education is beginning to reach a reasonable level.

The national centre and the Centre for Educational Theory and Information Technology (*Informatikcentre og Center for Pædagogik og Informatik*) procure and produce EDP programmes for educational use. All educators are the potential clientele of these organisations, rather than only adult educators. Indeed, this function is also fulfilled by the very few

Information Technology Centres which have been established in the country.

Centres for teachers in adult education (*Voksenpædagogiske Centre — VPC*)

The largest and most varied supplementary training facilities for youth and adult teachers are to be found at the centres for teachers of adult education, of which there are eight in Denmark. These centres run three types of course.

1 Professional courses, where teachers can be up-dated on the latest development within their field or topic. It may be a presentation of the latest fashion designs, which the sewing teachers may wish to teach in evening school, or an introduction to Caribbean music, or language-fluency courses for teachers who have little opportunity to practise their languages.
2 Methodology courses which deal with both the content and the method of teaching adults.
3 General courses in educational theory and practice. The centres have all tried to reach agreement, since they started in the 1970s, on an adult education training course of about 200 hours, but thus far have been without success. However, experiments are being conducted elsewhere and teacher qualifications are beginning to emerge. Teachers of adults must not only be inspiring teachers but they must also be educational counsellors, initiators and cultural workers.

Apart from the training activities these centres are in charge of experimental and developmental work and they also advise people who are themselves working on projects.

Finally, some courses are developments for adult education teachers and the outline below shows the type of thinking that is emerging in this country:

- Introduction: Status of educational theory and practice. What are we doing and why?
- Adult education outside adult education centres — personnel from outside the field of education show how they educate adults.
- Participants: Who are they?
                    How do adults learn?
- Teachers: Why are we teachers?

Who are the teachers?
What are the effects of teaching?
- Teachers and participants — meeting.
Teaching methods in adult education:
- Experience-orientated teaching.
- Communication in the classroom: both communication and transaction analysis.
- The sex distribution: discussion on the issues that arise from this.
- Non-verbal communication.
- Social networks in adult education.
- Evaluation of teaching.
- Adult education and the future: new frames/new contents?
- Suggestopedy and hypno-educational theory.
- Microteaching.
- Planning, implementation and evaluation of teaching.
- Projects and their presentation.

This is one course outline. Readers can judge how advanced such a course is, but it has to be seen in the light of the fact that adult education remains the one area in teaching in Denmark where there is no statutory requirement to have undertaken a course before employment.

14   The training of adult educators in Finland

Pentti Yrjölä

In order to understand the preparation of adult educators in Finland it is first necessary to understand the adult education system. The first section of this chapter is therefore devoted to outlining this necessary background.

THE FINNISH ADULT EDUCATION SYSTEM

The system of adult education in Finland is made up of different educational organisations and institutes which have developed at different times. We do not have a uniform system of adult education like the school system. We do have a rather multiform network of different kinds of organisations, so that it is not possible to discover a single type of adult educator.

In order to understand the system, the following outline is presented. It is constructed mainly on the basis of administrative structure.

- Liberal adult education: There are adult education centres, i.e. civic and workers' institutes, folk high schools and liberal education organisations having their own study centres.
- Vocational adult education: There are employment training in vocational course centres, schooling organised by employers, many kinds of vocational courses organised by vocational schools and colleges, summer universities and a variety of other organisations.
- Other forms of adult education: A variety of organisations, including universities, radio and television, private schools and colleges.

On the basis of a survey by the General Statistical Office of Finland about 26 per cent of the population over the age of fifteen years participated in adult education in 1980. About 16 per cent of all the adults studied in adult education centres while

Table 14.1 Classification of adult educators according to their position and duties

Category	Function – administrative, planning and organisational	Teaching functions
Full-time	Principals in folk high schools, adult education centres, study centres, vocational institutes and evening schools. Training managers and planners in the work place. Administrators, planners and researchers in public and private sectors.	Teachers and trainers in adult education schools, centres, institutes, organisations and universities.
Partial	Various kinds of jobs in industry and institutes where education constitutes less than 50% of the job. Some executive directors of voluntary organisations or personnel directors in the private sector.	Teaching in the organisations mentioned in the middle column.
Part-time	Adult education planning or administration done outside of normal working time.	Teachers, part-time, working on an hourly basis and study circle leaders (*animateurs*) not including those who lecture occasionally.

Table 14.2 The number of adult educators in 1986 (approx)

Category	Administration	Teaching	Total
Full-time	4,000	7,000	11,000
Partial	1,000	3,000	4,000
Part-time	1,000	56,000	57,000
Totals	6,000	66,000	72,000

the other 10 per cent participated in other forms of liberal adult education. About 13 per cent followed vocational courses while another 7 per cent studied in other courses organised by employers. Other forms of adult education had about 2 per cent of the population, but it is clear from these figures that there was considerable overlap.

The largest expansion in adult education in recent years has been that organised by employers; this growth appears destined to continue in the future.

THE NUMBER AND FUNCTIONS OF ADULT EDUCATORS

There are no exact figures about the number of adult educators in Finland because it is difficult to define who is an adult educator. In Table 14.1 a distinction is made between those who work full-time and those who are part time in some capacity. Full-time work naturally means that a person earns his/her living by working in adult education, over 50 per cent of the time being spent in either teaching or planning. Partial adult educators refers to those who have another full-time job and a smaller share of their time, i.e. under 50 per cent, is spent in adult education. The third category, the part-timers, are persons who only occasionally do some adult education work, i.e. give lessons, or guide study circles without payment. Other personnel, who might fall into this category of adult educators in other countries, such as social, health, religious or voluntary workers, are not considered to be so in Finland.

Table 14.2 provides only a rough estimate of the actual number of adult educators and it is based partly on the statistics of the National Board of General Education and partly on a personal estimate. However, it may be seen from the table that by far the greatest number of adult educators work part-time, but only a few of them have received any educational preparation for their work. During the past few years the standard of their andragogical knowledge has been raised, however, because their salaries in the adult education centres have been tied to their studies of adult education.

The andragogical basic education of full-time adult educators is also unsatisfactory because many of them have received no university education, neither in general nor in adult education. In the workplace vocational competence is much more important than andragogical ability, so that many of these adult educators have studied the engineering sciences, administrative or social studies at university. In the area of liberal adult education, the

165

requirements for getting a permanent job is an academic degree, studies in adult education or general education and practical training. These requirements are based upon the state subsidy laws in Finland. In any event, it may be said that a career in adult education is an exception. Many people perform these duties for a few years and then go into a normal 'vocational' career. It is also quite common to get a permanent job in adult education and to stay in the same position until retirement.

ADULT EDUCATION IN THE UNIVERSITIES

The Civic College, also known as the School of Social Sciences, began to educate workers for popular education as early as 1929 and the position of a part-time teacher was established for this purpose. By 1949 this teaching position became a professorship and later the School of Social Sciences moved to Tampere and its name changed to Tampere University. Today adult education is taught at all levels by the Department of Adult Education and Youth Work at Tampere University, and also now by the Department of Education at the University of Helsinki. There are, consequently, two universities where adult education is taught but there are actually eight universities where general education is taught.

Each year universities admit a total of about thirty students to programmes for the MA in adult education and about fifteen to twenty usually complete their studies. Adult education can also be taken as a minor subject and there are about 150 to 200 students a year who follow this. Additionally, it is possible to take university-level studies in the summer universities and a similar number of students study these courses each year.

During the year 1985-6 a series of programmes on the principles of the open university in adult education were broadcast on radio and television. Several thousand students took part in this but very few actually sat the examinations.

The programme in adult education is divided into three parts, as are all university study programmes in Finland: general studies, subject studies and specialist studies. The unit of study is one study week, which is the equivalent of about forty hours of full-time study and the whole programme consists of 160 study weeks, divided as follows:

1. *General studies (31 study weeks)*
- planning studies,
- man, nature and society,

- fundamentals of scientific activity,
- general studies in education,
- general studies in other sciences.

2. *Subject studies (93 study weeks)*
- administration and organisation of adult education,
- psychology of adult education,
- didactics of adult education,
- research in education and adult education,
- science of adult education,
- teaching practice,
- adult education, work and leisure.

3. *Specialist studies (36 study weeks)*
- functions of adult education in society,
- planning of adult education,
- methods of adult education research,
- specialist studies in the educational sciences.

These studies include compulsory reading, a great deal of group work and lectures.

The degree of Master of Education can be taken after about five years and the degree holder has the right to continue his/her studies for the degree of Licentiate in Education. The degree of Doctor of Education may be awarded on the basis of a successful dissertation.

It should be pointed out that the adult educator is required to have a working knowledge of the structure and organisation of society, and also knowledge of human behaviour both as an individual and as a member of a group. This is the reason why students receive basic knowledge in sociology, social psychology and psychology. However, the study of philosophy may be given too little attention. Because there is so much new knowledge in the social sciences available it is difficult for a university teacher, an adult education researcher or an adult educator to find his/her own way through the field.

QUALIFYING STUDIES IN LIBERAL ADULT EDUCATION

As indicated above, in order to get a permanent position in a folk high school or in an adult education centre the applicant must have a university degree, have studied adult education or general education and had special practical training for that position. This is because of the state subsidy law for the institutes. In the folk high schools there are ninety full-time principals, 610 teachers and 3,600 part-time teachers. In the adult education centres there are 280 full-time principals, 480 teachers and about 30,000 part-time teachers.

The practical training is planned and directed by a board which includes membership from the National Board of General Education, the folk high schools and the adult education centres. This training has been developed recently in a uniform manner so that a teacher is qualified to teach in both folk high schools and adult education centres. The training itself consists of a twelve-week orientation period on the functions of liberal adult education and a three-week period of courses and seminars during which the institutions are studied in much greater detail. During the training the teacher must give demonstration lectures and complete a reading list in adult education. Those who were trained before this joint system was introduced for either folk high schools or adult education centres are given the opportunity to acquire competence in the other system through a scheme of further study.

To be qualified for the position of principal the teacher must study administration, economics, planning and leadership techniques for ten weeks and also pass an examination on the administration of liberal adult education. It is also necessary for those who teach in evening schools to have a degree in secondary education. About 150 to 200 teachers and about 40 to 50 principals receive their degrees annually. All of the above statistics have been published in Finland by the National Board of General Education.

THE TRAINING OF ADULT EDUCATORS IN VOCATIONAL EDUCATION

There are forty-two vocational centres and ten course units for employment training. The course centres are intended for unemployed adults or for persons who are in danger of becoming unemployed. The centres function as part of official labour policy and are financed through the Ministry of Education. More than 37,000 students participate annually and these courses last from six to eight months. The centres themselves employ about 1,000 full-time teachers who are specialists in some occupation or vocation, and there are a further 700 who teach part-time. The full-time teachers are usually engineers by profession or have an MA, but very few of them have an MA in education or in adult education. About 70 per cent of them have studied a forty-week study unit in pedagogy or andragogy and they have undertaken a short period of practice training.

Within a few years the personnel from these centres will have the opportunity of taking a further training period of one week each year organised by a university, and this in-service training will be considered as part of their work.

Finnish industry and commerce has traditionally had its own vocational education institutes and about forty industrial enterprises do have such facilities which provide further training, based upon vocational secondary education. This training is mainly specialised for specific jobs and the training staff are predominantly specialist practitioners in their sphere of work.

On the vocational side, additionally, it may be seen that many people with adult education qualifications and experience have been recruited into the administrative and planning roles.

SPECIAL ARRANGEMENTS

During the last few years many kinds of projects and new ideas have been introduced in order to provide adult educators with more professional knowledge:

- Open University studies, connected with further education, universities or summer universities, have provided wider opportunities for working towards degrees.
- Two private organisations, the Adult Education Research Society and the Association of Training Managers, have both been active in providing opportunities to enlarge professional skills and the latter has achieved a significant position among training managers in the business world.
- In liberal adult education the national organisations service the needs of staff of the member institutes, i.e. study centres which are responsible for educating the leaders of study circles.
- A special institute, the State Training Centre, has been established for the training of civil servants, and this institute has also produced some new ideas that other fields of adult education might consider.
- Private organisations also provide training in personnel development, in the training of trainers, etc. but there is not a great deal of reliable information about these organisations.

THE INCREASING REQUIREMENTS OF
ADULT EDUCATORS

The process of professionalisation has been operative in the occupation of adult education within Finland during the past ten to fifteen years, a process which I think will continue. There are three areas in which a professional adult educator must be proficient:

- Professional skills — he/she must have a full knowledge of teaching content.
- Didactic skills of the subject being taught — he/she must be a specialist in the teaching of his/her own subject.
- Andragogical abilities, — he/she must have the ability to teach adults with a knowledge of the relevant social, psychological and pedagogical facts.

As a result of this process of professionalisation, the following new requirements for adult educators must now be specified:

- The ability to use and adapt new information technology.
- The social skills to be able to work in a group.
- Communication skills, including the use of foreign languages.
- A positive attitude towards continuous learning which, for adult educators means an active participation in a variety of different studies.

FOUR VIEWS OF THE PROFESSION

Professor Aulis Alanen (1988) has been concerned about the kind of images that adult educators have of their profession, the basic demands of the profession and the level at which the adult educator should work in order to be regarded as competent. Some theoreticians suggest that the adult educator must have a clear and internalised understanding of the aims and values of adult education — but what are they?

The following classification is aimed mainly at those adult educators who work within liberal adult education, but it can be adapted for other forms of adult education. In Alanen's opinion adult educators have four kinds of views about their profession.

The adult educator who has adopted humanistic values tries to follow these values and the educational principles that follow. The ideal profession may be called 'the promotion of intellectual-mental growth'. Two different approaches to this can be seen in as much as some have adopted this view quite emotionally whilst others have a more critical perspective. If the adult educator is a prisoner of his/her own ideology, then his/her views of the profession may be called a 'believer's view of mental growth', whereas if he/she is critical it may be referred to as a 'critical view of education'.

The above division is based upon a rationalisation of values but the following one is characterised by a rationalisation of targets. This is connected with the continuing professionalisation of adult education and the manner by which adult educators are becoming professional specialists. The profession is characterised by functional activity, by lack of interest in the aim of the actual work, by professional entrepreneurism and adaptation into the social system. This rationalism of targets can be divided into two: bureaucratic and marketing. In the former view of the profession its norms are important — the laws and regulations, the obedience of the civil servants, the needs of employers and all kinds of regulation and contract. This is the third view of the profession and may be called 'conscious job-holding'. In the fourth one, the marketing aspect, the adult educator's view of the profession is easy to define: it is about flexibility of demand and the development of a supply of adult educational services connected with the activation of participation. Important to this view is both the increase in volume and the market share of work — it may be called the 'effective service' model. This approach contains three features: an uncritical principle — 'let all the flowers flourish'; leaving the responsibility for choice and evaluation to the participants: appealing to a broad public interest for legitimation.

The principle of satisfaction of demand does not contribute a serious attempt to activate social criticism and distinguish it from a false radicalism, up-to-date superficiality and escapism — phenomena which are served by many kinds of salvation truth. Indeed, it is impossible in an objective manner to distinguish between which educational programmes are valuable and which are not. One basis for evaluation is the adult educator him/herself. However, persons with many kinds of values and with various motives have already been recruited into the profession. The development and formation of the profession is, at the same time, a process which can be influenced and educational consciousness can be developed but only by becoming acquainted with the basic facts of adult education.

This is one of the challenges for both basic and further education of adult educators. This type of consciousness of aims must be supported with knowledge of both the situation and the methods. Knowledge of the situation not only includes some specific vocational knowledge but also a realistic orientation towards society. Because of the formal qualifications for positions in liberal adult education it is possible to disseminate views about educational consciousness with the help of the universities. However, this is a very different matter in vocational adult education where it is hardly possible to imagine the development of this kind of view about the profession.

THE FUTURE

Two directions in which adult education might develop may be seen clearly at the present time. Vocational adult education will continue to grow and changes in content will occur depending upon changes in the circumstances in the world of work. The other change will be connected with the growth of free time and the way in which people use their leisure, which may result in changes in the content of adult education becoming more cultural with less emphasis upon the educational.

BIBLIOGRAPHY

Alanen, A. (1988) 'Efficient service as the professional ideal of adult educators', reprinted in *Adult Education in Finland*, no 4. pp. 2-13 which was first published in 1985 in *Humanistin Teetojen Tuntumah* Acta Universitatis Tamperen, series A, vol 196, pp. 134-50 (essays in honour of Professor Urpo Harva).

15   The training of adult educators in Norway

Hallgjerd Brattset

INTRODUCTION

Since the late 1950s the training of adult educators has been continuously discussed in Norway. This is closely related to the rapid expansion of the field in the post-war period. Leaders of adult education realised the needs for providing training for workers in the field, and thus also for establishing adult education as an academic discipline.

The term 'adult educator' is hardly used in Norway. Instead of a common, broad term, it is more usual to apply terms describing the different functions assumed: circle leader, teacher, instructor, adviser, organiser, administrator. The range of terms is a result of the expansion in the field, the division into sectors, combined with the fact that there are few opportunities for professional training for adult educators.

Because adult education is regarded as a marginal activity in the education system, the term applied to the middle of the 1960s was enlightenment; the discussions about its development were limited to adult education circles at that early stage. In addition, when it comes to training, the position of workers with teaching functions was recognised. Before discussing the present situation as regards training, it may, therefore, prove useful to consider briefly the development of and the present scene in adult education in Norway.

HISTORICAL BACKGROUND

The history of Norwegian adult education is closely linked with popular movements dating back until the last century. These movements and the voluntary organisations associated with them are inseparable phenomena. As a matter of fact, these voluntary organisations dominated the field of adult education until the 1960s, and their aims were to promote changes in society in accord with their values, so that their activities can only be described as instrumental. For this reason the study circle tradition has had a strong impact on the development of adult education in this country and this has affected the provision, educational approach and the prerequisite qualifications for adult educators. The principle of the study circle leader being *primus inter pares*, the first among equals, has to some extent permeated the thinking of adult education and has, therefore, influenced discussions on the training of educators in the field.

The developments, leading up to the Adult Education Act (1976), were also highly influenced by the voluntary organisations; they were in fact the most ardent supporters of the proposed law.

From the late 1950s and the early 1960s the scene of adult education changed. Among the new partners in adult education were now: school authorities, manpower authorities, organisations from the world of work. The concept of adult education has thus become more comprehensive. In addition, the authorities accepted responsibility for the development of the field as part of the educational system. Storting (Parliament) Proposition no 92 (1964-5), *On Adult Education Training*, approved by parliament in 1965, serves as an illustration of government policy in the period 1965 to 1976. Two principles of utmost importance were emphasised:

- Adult education should be on equal footing with basic education for children and young people.
- Adult education was seen as being both liberal and vocational.

Furthermore, the intentions of proposing an adult education act were announced, and the need for research and training for adult education was mentioned. The immediate results of parliament's approval of the proposition were:

- A special department of adult education in the Ministry of Church and Education was established in 1966.
- The first State Council of Adult Education, advisory to the Ministry, was appointed in 1966.
- Reforms in the examination system in primary and secondary education in 1968 made it easier for adults to achieve formal qualifications at these levels.
- Public grants towards provision of adult education increased.

The outcome of this was increased recruitment to all sectors of the field; the voluntary organisations still maintained a strong position among the providers and they also extended their activities to include examination courses and courses for the general public, as well as their own members, which had not been their previous practice.

THE ADULT EDUCATION ACT

A committee to work out a proposal for an act of adult education was appointed in 1970; the Ministry's proposition was presented to the Storting in 1975 and became law in 1976. It was operative from August 1977 and consists of the following main principles:

- The mere existence of the Act is important. Legislation represents a recognition of the field and puts adult education on an equal footing with other parts of the educational system.
- The Act does not establish a right to adult education.
- The Act only provides for financial contributions towards the provision of adult education from the state.
- Decisions are left to the appropriate governing bodies, e.g. regional and local.
- The Act gives priority to special groups, i.e. disadvantaged adults, aiming at providing equality of access to education.
- Basic education at all levels is financed completely by the authorities.
- In order to be recognised and approved by the Ministry of Church and Education, and consequently entitled to state grants, organisations and institutions within all sectors of the field must have an educational practice which gives participants, as a group, reasonable influence on the content and methods in their group.

With the exception of the final statement, the Act has no special regulations concerning the educational approach, required qualifications by the staff or provisions for training. Adult education is not only, however, governed by this Act; it is also regulated by several other educational acts, depending on the sector/level concerned. Within the scope of the Act, the responsibility for providing adult education is mainly divided between voluntary organisations, school authorities, manpower authorities and occupational organisations.

Examples of the provisions outside of the scope of the Act are in-service training (basic and further education) in the civil service, in the armed forces (liberal and vocational training), training within industry and the other occupational organisations. Provisions are mainly vocational. They are either financed from the ordinary budgets of various ministries or from funds from foundations established especially for the purpose by regular contributions from both employers and employees.

The distinction between adult education within and outside the scope of the law is felt to be artificial to some extent, as is the division into sectors within the two areas. Despite variations in legal, financial and organisational measures, it is felt that there is a need to consider the whole field as a unity, to meet demands and solve problems which are common to all sections. Two committees have been appointed by the government which serve as examples of this:

- A committee to consider the effects of implementing a system of lifelong learning was established in 1981 and presented its report in 1987. The Ministry of Church and Education is now preparing a report which will go to parliament, based upon its findings.
- A committee to propose certification of knowledge and skills for adults without formal qualifications was established in 1982 and the first report of this committee was presented to the Ministry of Church and Education in 1985.

RESEARCH AND DEVELOPMENT WORK IN ADULT EDUCATION

Government policy in the period from 1965 to 1976 was not, however, limited to establishing a legal and financial basis for the development of adult education. Two more proposals of importance to the qualitative work of the field were presented to, and approved by, the Storting. They were proposals to establish two national institutions, funded directly by the Ministry of Church and Education: the Norwegian Institute of Adult Education, established in 1976, and the Norwegian State Institution for Distance Education, established in 1977. The former is concerned with research, documentation and information but has no training functions, apart from providing advice to the providers of such training. The reports from the Institute do, however, meet the demands for relevant literature in the training of adult educators. The latter is a providing body, co-operating with other partners in the field in projects developing material, chiefly multi-media courses, and organising and evaluating courses for adults. Included in this work is counselling part-time workers involved in organising various local projects.

THE PRESENT SITUATION IN NORWEGIAN ADULT EDUCATION

We have now had ten years of experience of the Adult Education Act but one complicating factor in assessing its effects is that the economic situation has changed very much since it became operative and in a manner contrary to expectations at that time.

Provisions for and recruitment to adult education had increased steadily before the Act came into operation and continued to do so in the first years of its existence. This was no doubt due to the improved economic conditions within all sectors of adult education. This development increased the need for staff, and a considerable number of new positions, both full-time and part-time, were established. However, it is probable that the number of full-time workers employed never actually exceeded 20 per cent of the total workforce — in 1965 it was estimated as 8 per cent.

With the new economic conditions this trend has changed. For example, participants' contributions towards course fees in voluntary organisations have increased during the period 1979 to 1985 from 20 per cent to nearly 77 per cent of the total costs. This has affected recruitment. Compared to 1981, the 1982 statistics of the Norwegian Association of Adult Education Organisations show a decrease of 10 per cent, which is about 100,000 study circle members. Naturally this has had an effect on the number of positions in the field and, apart from industry, no new positions have been established in recent years. Indeed, within other sectors there has actually been a decrease.

Decisions on the provision are, as already mentioned, left to the appropriate regional and local bodies. Contributions from local authorities, both counties and municipalities, vary since the Act does not stipulate their contribution. This also applies to adult basic education since there is a sharing of costs between state, region and municipality as in the education of the young. This means that basic education will only be provided and completely financed by the authorities, according to the regulations, when the regional or local body decides that there is a need for it. Their divisions may very well be influenced by their own financial situation. For instance, there is evidence that densely populated municipalities, with well-educated inhabitants and comfortable financial and administrative resources, have made more provision for adult education than those less prosperous areas.

The Ministry of Church and Education has presented two White Papers to parliament since the law became operative: in 1981 (Storting Proposition no 72, 1980-81) and, after the change in government, in 1984 (Storting Proposition no 43, 1984-5). In the former training for adult educators was mentioned as one of the priorities for the coming years. The present policy is to give priority to adult basic education, both liberal and vocational, and to disadvantaged groups, such as handicapped persons, persons with little basic education, those with heavy family obligations and also to immigrants and refugees.

ADULT EDUCATORS IN NORWAY

There is no way of knowing how many adult educators there are in Norway and, indeed, the fact that this information does not exist indicates that the focus has been on provision and recruitment rather than on collecting statistics. However, there is every reason to believe that Houle's (1960) conception of a pyramid as a description of the relationship between the functions and numbers of adult educators is also valid for Norway. At the base we find the largest number, the part-timers, volunteers, etc., whilst in the middle we find a smaller group who combine adult education with other duties as part of their employment. Finally, at the apex of the pyramid is the smallest group composed of the specialists who have adult education as their main concern.

A general picture of workers in adult education is given below:

- The majority are part-timers.
- Most have teaching functions, but without always having had teacher training. Only a few have training in adult education.
- Their links with adult education are rather tenuous since most have other kinds of full-time employment. Their links with the field may also be temporary, partly due to the changing needs of the population.
- Normally they have one or two courses per week and their average number of hours of employment rarely exceeds six.
- They have few offers of training and guidance and few opportunities to exchange experiences and to discuss problems. In many cases they feel isolated in their situation.

- Their conditions of work vary in relation to the sector in which they are employed and even their fees are decided locally by the employing agency. Since they do not represent a homogeneous group of workers, they have no special union to take care of their interests.
- Their links with adult education do not generally give them any status.

These characteristics do, however, require some elaboration:

- Some part-timers combine administrative and teaching functions.
- Local organisers (part-time and full-time) in voluntary organisations usually have previous experience in study circles.
- Full-time workers in all sectors normally hold administrative/organisational positions.
- Recruitment to the full-time staff is usually from the part-timers.

Finally, it should be taken into consideration that these characteristics apply mainly to workers who are active in providing adult education. The pattern is not so clear when it comes to researchers and teachers in universities and institutions of higher education, or to personnel who combine the normal duties of their full-time employment with tasks in adult education, e.g. information giving, counselling. It is more difficult to describe the upper levels of Houle's pyramid. From this it follows that we have two sets of main categories of adult educators, depending upon either their links to or their functions in the field: full-time and part-time workers, administrators or teachers. As already mentioned, the majority of full-time workers have administrative/organisational duties, while part-timers, on the whole, have teaching duties.

NEEDS FOR TRAINING

With the wide range of workers in the field needs will, naturally, vary. Training needs will relate to the roles and functions of those who are engaged in adult education work but will also relate to the expectations that the workers have of being engaged in adult education in the future. It is only right to state that most workers, especially the part-timers, do not identify themselves with the field. To them their engagement is a marginal activity and they do not fully recognise that they are part of a national, even international, field.

However, when asked, workers do admit that they need guidance and training, as the findings of a survey conducted in the voluntary organisations in 1978 shows. Study circle leaders were concerned with the wide distribution of knowledge, skills, interests, needs and study techniques among circle members, combined with their own lack of training in adult education. This means that they experience central aims in the Adult Education Act, participants' influence, as concrete educational problems. Organisers agree with this and mention their own problems: lack of competent study circle leaders, insufficient capacity to contact and guide the leaders combined with their own feeling of lack of competence in adult education (Brattset 1984). The organisers obviously regard this as a problem and recognise that giving advice and support to study circle leaders (part-timers) ought to be a part of their regular duties. In the same study, it was estimated that in 1981 some 40,000 study circle leaders and 1,400 local organisers were in need of some kind of counselling or training in the voluntary organisation. There is reason to believe that the situation is similar in other sectors of the field.

QUALIFICATIONS REQUIRED FOR ADULT EDUCATORS

The need felt for training for adult education is obviously to some extent related to the qualifications required. The Adult Education Act, as previously mentioned, does not specify any qualifications for adult education workers, regardless of role or function. The Ministry of Church and Education has left it to individual voluntary organisations to decide upon which qualifications should be required, stating that the aims and content of the courses should govern the selection of study circle leaders. The appointments are, therefore, left to the local organisers. The findings from the survey of voluntary organisations show that their criteria for selection are: experience of applying the subject in practice, the ability to relate to people, knowledge, skills and teaching experience. Emphasis is upon practical rather than formal qualification and this corresponds most closely with what might be expected from the traditions of the organisations.

There are similar regulations to the voluntary organisations for the work-related provision, which is funded by the state. However, in basic and vocational adult education teaching qualifications are required, relating to the educational level taught, e.g. primary, secondary. Folk high schools, which function under a separate act, normally require degrees in the relevant subject or a teaching certificate. At university level no teacher training is required and this also applies to other sectors of adult education which lie outside the scope of the Act, such as the training of civil servants. This means that no special competence in adult education is required, for provision in neither non-formal nor formal adult education whether it is within the scope of the Act, or not. Competence, i.e. training and practical experience, in the subject is the decisive factor in the selection of adult education teaching staff.

The situation is similar when it comes to recruitment of personnel with career expectations in all sectors of the field, i.e. the full-timers in administrative or organisational positions. A study of the advertisements for these positions reveals this. Some mention might be made about an interest in the subject being desirable. This relates to adult education as an academic discipline and its training opportunities.

THE TRAINING OF ADULT EDUCATORS

The first opportunity for training of a professional character was established in 1970 at Oslo University, where certificates have been awarded since 1981. Until then activities in this area had mostly been limited to short courses for part-time workers with teaching functions, mainly in the voluntary organisations.

Adult education and the role of universities

Adult education as an academic discipline has not had a long tradition in Norway, indeed it is post-war, and is still not firmly established in either universities nor colleges of higher education. There is, for instance, no chair of adult education in the country. In fact, the Norwegian Institute of Adult Education, founded in 1976, is the first institution established with research, documentation and consultative services as its objectives. It is funded directly by the Ministry of Church and Education. Little research was conducted before the Institute commenced its activities, probably because there has never been a close relationship between adult education and the universities in Norway. Moreover, university extension, which stimulates the academic discipline in other countries, is not part of the

Norwegian adult education tradition, although there have been links between the organisations and academics interested in the field and its institutions.

Training opportunities

There are few formally recognised training opportunities that are both permanent and professional at an academic level in Norway. The number of courses has, in fact, been reduced in recent years from five in 1981 (four run in the universities or colleges in Oslo, Bodø, Trondheim and Rauland and one organised by the Norwegian Association of Employers) to only one in 1986 run at Oslo. The Oslo course alone offers certification, which it has since 1981, and then only on specific conditions.

Teacher training colleges may organise a course in adult education, equivalent to six months' study, as further education for teachers. However, only two such courses have been organised since 1976 because of low recruitment. Yet the target group has been teachers in the folk high schools. Other colleges include adult education in their professional training. Librarians, for instance, were the first to include it, and also secondary school teachers training; vocational and personnel officer training both include it.

To do justice to the whole range of workers in the field, we would also take into account the short-term courses and seminars for persons engaged in adult education part-time. In this context training as a term is more rightly replaced by such terms as guidance and counselling. Most of these courses, which are not part of a regular and systematic programme, are run internally by organisations and institutions for their own purposes. Teacher training colleges occasionally run short courses for part-timers at the initiative of providers from the local communities.

The framework of these short courses is governed by financial resources for which the part-timers can apply. Organisations may apply to the Ministry of Church and Education for financial support for courses of this nature but there are only limited resources and even these have been reduced since 1979. In addition, there are travel study grants for which adult educators may apply. However, the same restricted conditions exist and these have also been reduced.

Table 15.1 Training and guidance in voluntary organisations

Type of guidance	%
Advisory talk	55.6
Meeting with leaders	18.5
Written instructions	14.6
Short course	7.6
Other counselling	3.7

TRAINING OPPORTUNITIES RELATED TO NEEDS

Related to the estimated amount of need, opportunities for training and guidance are scarce in Norway. This applies to workers in all parts of the field, whether full-time or part-time, or whether they are teachers or planners and organisers. In a survey of the voluntary organisations, for instance, less than 50 per cent of the study circle leaders stated that they had received any guidance before they started their work. Table 15.1 highlights the findings.

It appears from Table 15.1 that the most frequent form of guidance is an individual chat with a leader. Training courses are not really mentioned, although 3.7 per cent say that they have attended a short course as a part-timer. This is naturally related to the provision available. The lack of trainers is one reason given for insufficient opportunities for guidance of part-timers with teaching functions. Few in adult education combine practical experience in the field with training for that purpose. Indeed, the leaders themselves say that they do not always have the capacity to give guidance. The lack of trainers is one result of there being an insufficient number of places on the university-level courses. A total of less than 600 have been admitted since the first course was arranged in 1970.

These courses are part-time and equivalent to one year's full-time study. Only two of them have run regularly throughout the whole period and while they are organised differently they do have a similar target group, that is students with experience in adult education. The majority of these have been full-time workers with administrative tasks. The reason for this is that full-time workers are able to get paid leave, while the part-time staff with other full-time work will obviously not be in a

Table 15.2 Recruitment to studies in adult education 1970-81

Type of organisation	%
Industry	36.1
Civil service	19.7
Voluntary organisations	18.5
Public education system	10.5
Correspondence schools	1.4
No information	8.9
Other organisations	3.8
No links with adult education	1.1

position to obtain this so easily. Recruitment is, as shown in Table 15.2, from all sections of the field but it has increasingly come from those parts that lie outside the scope of the Adult Education Act.

The conclusion that can be drawn from this discussion is that opportunities for training and guidance in Norway at present are mainly aimed at those who are already at work in the field and that these are not sufficient to meet the estimated demands. Apart from academic studies in adult education, which are not extensive, hardly any provision exists for potential adult educators. Where there is provision, few use it and this is a consequence of the lack of appropriate regular courses.

The nature of the courses in adult education

Entrance qualifications to part-time study in adult education at university in Norway relate to experience in the field or the practice of teaching. The institutions have waived other formal requirements for admitting students to these studies, which means that the courses are of the nature of in-service training or further education for full-time workers with administrative or planning responsibilities. It also means that students will only receive a certificate in adult education if they meet the requirements of ordinary university entrance qualifications, pass the examination in some additional courses and have otherwise completed the courses satisfactorily. The only credit course so far run is organised by the Institute of Educational Research at the University of Oslo, where it started in 1981. The content of this course is interdisciplinary and includes: psychology, education, sociology, history, philosophy, the organisation of adult education and comparative education. With the exception of courses intended for clearly defined target groups, such as training in vocational adult education, methods and teaching techniques are only dealt with in a general way, so that they serve the planners best and, consequently, attract them from all levels.

The short courses provided for part-time adult educators are also intended for people already in work and they usually focus upon teaching and planning functions without being related to any particular methods that might be associated with any particular subject.

FUTURE NEEDS FOR TRAINING AND GUIDANCE

From the above description it follows that there are training needs within all sectors of adult education since the existing opportunities do not meet with the estimated demands. This brings us to the needs of the present situation and the potential target groups. Primarily this calls for an expansion of the existing opportunities for training, intended for people at work in the nature of in-service and further education and guidance. The two main categories of staff in this connection are:

- Administrators and organisers (full-time) with planning provision as part of their duties, as well as training and counselling of teachers and study circle leaders (part-time) at work.
- Study circle leaders and teachers (part-time), including those involved in adult basic education and in activities for the disadvantaged.

Obviously these two categories are not totally separate and an increase in the number of trained administrators will automatically improve the conditions of support for the part-timers. The more who can undertake this course, the sooner the lack of trainers will be eliminated.

In addition to this, there is the need for training opportunities for another group, the potential adult educators with career expectations. The lack of regular courses for this category is a likely reason why so few people specialise in adult education as part of their university studies. Closely related to this is the demand to include adult education in the training of other professions such as social workers, health personnel and information workers.

In addition, there is a need to relate the content of the courses to the roles and functions of those who undertake the practical work. Emphasis upon counselling has already been mentioned, but for teachers there is a considerable need to expand the time devoted to methods and teaching techniques, especially for those part-timers who have had no previous teaching experience. Theoretically the variety of needs for training and guidance call for an increase in the number of specialised courses. From a practical point of view, however, with a small population of only four million scattered over an area similar in size to the United Kingdom, pragmatism must rule when it comes to the provision of training. Consequently, it is not possible at present to divide workers in the field into too many categories for training purposes. A possible benefit from this may be improved communication between groups of staff who work in different sectors of the field.

PROBLEMS

The formal recognition of adult education as an integral part of the Norwegian educational system is historically very recent. The Adult Education Act (1976) represents an important step in the right direction. Legal measures, however, are not sufficient. In times of economic constraint there are indications that attitudes towards adult education are less favourable than to other parts of the education system. One reason for this is that the idea that education is a lifelong phenomenon has not yet permeated the thinking of sufficient people for them to recognise the importance of adult education. Another reason is that compared to other sectors of the education service, professionalisation is only just beginning in adult education. This may be indicated by the following points:

- The proportion of full-time workers compared to part-timers is small.
- There are no definite requirements for competence for full-time workers in adult education.
- Training opportunities for professional, as well as adult educators at work, are few.
- Adult educators have no union to care for their professional interest.

From this it follows that in the long-term planning there is a need to discuss and settle the qualification requirements that we are placing upon various types of work. There is also a demand to quantify the places that we need for future professional training and to work out a tentative national scheme for establishing training at a university level. Future developments in the field no doubt depend upon a core of professionals who identify themselves with adult education, both nationally and internationally. To achieve this it is necessary to discuss with universities and colleges of higher education the future position of adult education as an academic discipline and, therefore, their role in the future development of training of adult educators.

PRESENT SITUATION — FUTURE DEVELOPMENT

At present there is a growing interest in the training and guidance of adult educators in Norway, as illustrated by:

- The Ministry of Church and Education, in its report to parliament in 1981, lists training of adult educators as one of its priorities in a follow-up to the Adult Education Act. It has approached the State Council of Teacher Training about this.
- Integration of adult education in the regular course of education in the teacher training colleges is at present being discussed.
- The Norwegian Association of Adult Education Organisations has worked out a scheme of short courses for study circle leaders in voluntary organisations; pilot courses are at present being organised.
- The number of reports from research and development work in adult education which place value on training and guidance for practitioners has increased in recent years.
- Teaching material, especially designed for adults and including multi-media courses produced by the Norwegian State Institution for Distance Education, has developed to a larger extent than previously.
- The number of people interested in training in all sectors of the field is increasing, judging from the numbers of the applications.
- The Norwegian Association of Secondary School Teachers plans to establish a special section for adult educators, teachers involved in adult basic education, in order to promote their interests.

All of this is part of the efforts to improve the quality of adult education and, hence, to strengthen the prestige of the field. The crucial question is, however, how to achieve an increase in the provision for training and guidance in order to meet the present demands. In this situation the need is obvious for initiatives and united efforts from organisations and institutions responsible for adult education provision, training and research.

BIBLIOGRAPHY

Houle, C.O. (1960) 'The education of educational leaders', in M.S. Knowles *Handbook of Adult Education in the United States*, Washington: Adult Education Association of the USA.

16 Training adult educators in Sweden

Yngve Kasimir

BACKGROUND: ADULT EDUCATION IN SWEDEN

Swedish adult education can be divided into non-formal adult education (NF) and formal adult education (FA). The former includes the folk high schools (FHS), which are mostly residential colleges of either a long-term or a short-term nature, the study circle associations (SCA) and the educational work undertaken by the different popular movements. The latter includes municipal adult education (MAE — Swedish 'Komvux') which comprises literacy classes and labour-market training (Swedish AMU). This provides a very broad overview of a rather complicated system.

HISTORY

Swedish non-formal adult education was a precondition of the growth of a democratic society as well as the fruit thereof. In the 1860s there was a radical change in the Swedish political system, both on a national and a local level and in both cases the farmers emerged as the dominant group. They needed training and education for their new tasks and since many Swedes had heard about the Danish folk high schools the idea was transferred to the new situation in Sweden, with the first three starting in 1868.

In the latter half of the nineteenth century Swedish industry, and concomitantly the number of industrial workers, started to grow rapidly. Towards the end of the century the Social Democratic Party, as well as the Trade Union Council (LO), were organised. Industrialisation also created a need and an opening for other popular movements, above all the temperance movement and the free churches. Many of the popular movements engaged themselves in adult education. The modern study circle, for instance, was born in 1902, and the National Study Circles Associations followed, with that of the Workers' Educational Association commencing in 1912.

The folk high schools were centres for democratic development in the country, but they were also disseminators of the new technology and fresh methods in agriculture. As new groups entered the folk high schools, or started their own schools, the agricultural training courses were separated from the general work of the folk high schools. They gave education and training to members and leaders of the popular movements and they also provided an opening to new jobs and to higher education. For a long period the folk high school was an alternative to formal secondary school; the demand for this kind of education for adults grew rapidly and could not be met by either the folk high schools or the study circle associations unless they changed and lost their non-formal adult education character.

In 1968 municipal adult education started its first courses, offering higher and primary education to adults. The number of courses and participants grew rapidly with some, albeit temporary, effect on the recruitment to both study circles and folk high schools.

In addition, to meet growing unemployment, however low compared to other countries, labour-market training, i.e. vocational training and re-training, was offered to adults who had lost their jobs or were in danger of so doing. Labour-market training also assumed a more general adult education role when this was required as a basis for the provision of vocational courses and, currently, such training has in excess of 100 residential training centres.

Finally, there were two other branches of adult education initiated in this country in the 1960s. The first was adult basic education (literacy and numeracy, etc.) required by a great number of immigrants from countries with high illiteracy rates. However, it soon became apparent that there were many Swedes, at least several tens of thousands, who also needed adult basic education and so it is now organised within municipal adult education and has approximately the same number of students as those enrolled in long-term courses within the folk high schools. The second is Swedish for Immigrants, which was established as an experiment in 1967, as a special task for the study circle associations. This is really the result of the heavy immigration that occurred in the 1960s and 1970s. Swedish for Immigrants has grown very rapidly and this expansion has placed a great strain upon organisers and staff.

Table 16.1 Adult education in Sweden

Non-formal adult education	Number of participants
Folk High School, courses of 15 weeks or more	17,000
Folk high school, short courses	230,000
Study circles	2,500,000
Formal adult education	
Municipal adult education	355,000
Labour-market training	120,000

Note: Total population of Sweden: 8,300,000.

FUTURE DEVELOPMENTS

In 1984 a report was published in Sweden on the effects of these changes. One of the main findings was that all forms of adult education, whether formal or non-formal, found great difficulties in reaching those who have received the least and the most inadequate previous education, and yet they were the priority target for most of the reforms that have occurred. Adult education has not lessened the educational gap between people. However, those who have participated in adult education have benefited; they have found better jobs and had grown more active culturally. The report recommended a redistribution of government grants so that those adult education associations which really recruited the disadvantaged should receive a greater proportion. It is still unclear as to whether such a decision will be taken but the report has caused a great deal of discussion within adult education about fundamental issues. There are also signs that all the political parties will give growing support to adult education when Sweden's financial situation permits it. Part of this support might be directed towards qualitative development, including staff development and research.

The greater proportion of the cost for full-time, and other more comprehensive adult education, is related to study grants to participants, since it is generally accepted in this society that adult education participation should be possible for everyone. A new government committee has been appointed to investigate funding arrangements for adult education. The size of the undertaking might be best understood from the statistics in Table 16.1.

EDUCATION OF ADULT EDUCATORS

From the historical survey given above it is evident that adult education until the 1960s was predominantly of the non-formal kind, with freedom from national and local governmental interference being very important. Those who were considered the most suitable candidates for jobs, for instance, by the organisations and the boards of the folk high schools, would get them. Good education and membership of the relevant organisations were the most important criteria for teaching, rather than formal teacher training. All the same, many formally trained teachers did become Study Circle Association study circle leaders and folk high school teachers. A training programme for primary school teachers was implemented shortly after compulsory primary education was introduced into Sweden, but a comprehensive training programme for secondary school teachers was not introduced until 1968, and at the same time a programme for the training of adult educators was also being discussed.

The need for a special training programme for adult educators

The discussions on this question have had two major concerns: the first of these considers adult education as distinct from child education and the second is focused upon training on the job, inside the organisations themselves, as opposed to authorised teacher training institutes or special service training programmes.

Training on the job or in special institutes

Both the Study Circle Associations and the folk high school movement have provided in-service, or on-the-job training for quite a long time, offering short courses of between two days and a week. At least in latter years the Study Circle Associations have been large enough to organise their own teaching staff training separately. The folk high schools, on the other hand, were forced into co-operation by their lack of size. The responsibility for teacher training here has been assumed by the teachers' trade union, i.e. the Swedish Union of Folk High School Teachers and Principals — SFHL. Using funds of its own, or supported by the schools or by government — county and municipality — it has organised short training courses. In addition, from the end of the 1950s the union and the Swedish National Board of Education co-operated to offer an annual course of four to five weeks' duration; this became the main training opportunity for young folk high school teachers during the 1960s. The union also pointed out, at an early stage, that more substantial training programmes were needed for teachers of adults. The need for an institution offering a training programme for adult educators was more strongly felt amongst the folk high school staff than amongst the staff of the Study Circle Associations. However, the above course was generally accepted at that time but a number of fears surfaced: that a common teacher training programme would force an unwanted type of uniformity upon the folk high schools and that those who came from a variety of other educational backgrounds would not be admitted to teacher training programmes regulated by the government.

The need for a special adult education teacher training programme?

The majority of folk high school teachers met the requirements for admission to the training programme for secondary school teachers that began in 1968, but this was aimed at youth education in a rather rigid system with a centrally decided curriculum.

In the case of the municipal adult education (Komvux) there was hardly any discussion about this issue in the 1960s. The reason for this appears to have been the rather limited programme that was organised, without any full-time staff of its own. The staff of Komvux comprised mainly primary and secondary school teachers who were undertaking a second job part-time, since the government regulations stipulated that Komvux teachers, and those teaching in labour-market training, had to have either completed a teacher training college course for primary school teachers or to have completed secondary school teacher training. This regulation had the support of the teachers' trade union.

When the adult basic education programme was introduced in 1977, there was no such discussion about the formal qualifications of the teaching staff. A large group of adult educators without any formal qualifications was involved; these were often persons who were strongly committed to the cause of the underprivileged, immigrants and the handicapped. The teachers' trade union, however, succeeded in bringing about a change, so that only those who were qualified in teaching children to read and write should teach in adult basic education.

Thus the special needs and conditions of the adult learner were not taken into account. This may have occurred because there were a decreasing number of pupils in primary school and a large number of teachers would have lost their jobs hence priority was given to them. This development was viewed by many, including both school leaders and immigrant organisations, as a negative factor in the development of an educational programme aimed at the personal development and the acquisition of knowledge and skills necessary for adult life. A government commission in 1982 also specified that there should be a special training programme for teachers in adult basic education. In 1985 parliament decided that such a programme should be offered, but merely as an option within primary school teacher training, or as an additional course after completing primary school teacher training. This means that even in the future the teachers who teach adults to read and write are basically trained to teach children.

There has not yet been any discussion in municipal adult education about introducing a course of training especially for adult educators. However, the labour-training market did receive a new and more independent structure on 1st January 1986 in which it was possible to expect special training and qualifications to teach adults from candidates for this form of work. Indeed, a special training programme may be developed for staff in this sector of education which is independent of, or additional to, the primary school programme referred to above.

Thus it may be seen from the above discussion that at the present time all teacher training for teachers of adults in formal adult education is based upon school teacher training. However, this has not been the case with non-formal adult education.

There were many claims in the folk high school sector that it required a special teacher training programme for its teaching staff since the aims and objectives of the movement are different from those of primary and secondary schools. There is certainly a greater variety and flexibility in courses and target groups in this movement. Above all there has been a consensus about the needs of teachers who are able to meet adult students and to be co-planners with them in the educational process since their needs are quite different from those of children and young people in ordinary schools.

This argument has been successful and an act of parliament established a special teacher training programme for teachers in folk high schools at the Teacher Training College at Linköping in 1970, as an alternative, or an option, within the secondary school teacher training programme. The same act also specified that an alternative sub-programme should be introduced within the Stockholm Teacher Training College secondary school course for the municipal adult education of the Komvux kind.

Both decisions meant that adult educators were to be trained within the framework of programmes preparing school teachers and it was not until 1977 that the folk high school programme was recognised as an independent programme. The Stockholm programme has remained as a sub-programme of the school teacher programme as before. As a whole, the weight given to adult education in teacher training has in no way been comparable to that of youth and child education. This is a remarkable fact when it is recognised that Sweden has a long history of adult education and a great number of adult students, indeed more than there are young people in secondary schools.

Swedish authorities now stress the importance of a broad curriculum in teacher training in order to incorporate a variety of possible groups of students, and also to prevent the possibility of having unemployed specialist teachers. This has not resulted, until now at least, in any substantial change in the unsatisfactory situation that has been described thus far. Indeed, in 1986 the Swedish government passed an act on qualifications for teachers of Swedish for young and adult immigrants which included no demands for any training in adult education.

TRAINING ADULT EDUCATORS TODAY

Within the government system

The folk high school teacher training programme

In 1970 the folk high school teacher training programme began at what was then the Teacher Training College at Linköping, where it was integrated into the training of secondary school teachers and where it was expected to operate within the same regulatory framework. It was also envisaged that the two groups of students should work together for a considerable part of their course. However, although the folk high school programme was allowed to differ in some respects it was generally agreed that it did not produce the type of results that it might have had had it been given autonomy to plan for its own needs. In 1977, when there was a total reform of the whole educational system in Sweden this separation occurred and the folk high school programme gained its own governing board under the umbrella of the University of Linköping's Teacher Training Department. This board makes decisions on content and organisation of the programme and has among its membership one-third teaching staff, one-third students and one-third from those organisations concerned with the folk high school movement, such as the Swedish Trade Union Council, the Association of County Administrations and the Swedish Federation of Non-Formal Adult Education Associations (*Folkbildningsförbundet*).

For admission to the folk high school programme two alternative sets of criteria are specified although, in fact, most students actually meet both sets.

1   To have completed a university programme of at least three years' duration, e.g. to hold a bachelor's degree, or
2   To have been working full-time for at least five years in adult education, or adult education administration in folk high schools, study circle associations or in any other association with special interests in adult education.

Each year there have been at least three times, and indeed as many as six times, as many applicants as there are places (seventy-five per annum). As a part of the admission procedure all qualified applicants are interviewed and given additional information about the course in order to avoid, as far as is possible, later disappointment. However, the regulations that give additional advantage to those who have experience in adult education practice means that almost everybody accepted in the programme is at least thirty-five years of age when they enter. The composition of age and experience in the student group certainly influences the working methods of the programme and, indeed, it is desirable that the methods used on the course should themselves be relevant to normal folk high school and other non-formal adult education work. The methods, therefore, tend to be non-academic in many respects. The programme consists of: pedagogics/andragogics, didactics, methodology and supervised teaching practice.

It is assumed that the student will have completed studies in his/her teaching subject prior to entry on the course, which extends over one academic year (forty weeks and forty credits) and is divided into four main blocks.

1   *Non-formal adult education*: its role in society, in Sweden and in other countries; the aims and objectives of different non-formal adult education organisations; methods in non-formal adult education; special target groups. This is a six-week (six-credit) course and also includes one week in a practical placement.

2 *Pedagogics/methodology*: this includes general studies in education, with some international perspectives; andragogy; general methodology; communication and media; introduction to research and development work. This is a fourteen-week block, six weeks of which are supervised teaching in non-formal adult education.

3 *Supervised teaching practice*: this is chosen in relevant fields of adult education in order to fill the gaps in previous experience, so that those who have had many years working in non-formal adult education, for instance, may choose to teach in a formal adult education setting, or in special branches such as educational broadcasting or television.

4 *Individualised block*: This consists of four weeks in option courses chosen from within a comprehensive programme organised by the academic staff of the course, in conjunction with the In-service Training Department, and is open to both the students and to teachers in the field of non-formal adult education. This is also worth four credits and includes the submission of a paper reporting upon some form of development in which the student has participated. In addition, there are a further fourteen credits which may be acquired by either theoretical or practical work, including supervised teaching for between one and six weeks, depending upon the student's previous experience, needs and interests.

The academic teaching staff on this course are either trained researchers in andragogy/pedagogy or else they are experienced field workers from relevant areas of non-formal adult education.

Within municipal adult education (Komvux)

At the Teacher Training College in Stockholm there is a special sub-programme within the secondary school teacher programme orientated to adult education. On the whole, students on this programme follow the same curriculum as do those who are preparing for work in youth education. However, certain parts of the course in pedagogics, methodology and teaching practice are geared to adult education.

The full programme covers four years and twenty-five students are admitted per annum. Three of the four years of this course comprise studies in the academic subject that the student is going to teach, while the pedagogical training covers only one year, forty credits, which is the same as for the non-formal adult education courses described above.

Private (non-governmental) programmes

The Trade Union Council training programme for adult educators

The Swedish Trade Union Council (LO), which is concerned traditionally with blue-collar workers, has established a training programme of its own in order to prepare for andragogical/pedagogical work in trade union education and in the folk high schools belonging to the labour movement. The training programme's profile is in accord with the ideas and goals of both labour and trade union movements. The programme aims at developing the participants' capacity for team-work and co-operation in general, developing their judgement and making them aware of their own attitudes and values. Important content in the course includes educational planning, practical teaching, leadership, administration in different kinds of educational situations and also follow-up activities.

The programme consists of three parts: theory, practice and a written paper. In total, the programme covers forty weeks, sixteen of which are devoted to theory. This is a course of pedagogics, methods and organisation of adult education, communication, introduction to the use of different media used in education (e.g. textbooks, television, field studies, etc.), research methods and evaluation. Fourteen weeks are given to teaching practice, undertaken predominantly on courses organised by the trade union movement or by individual unions. The other ten weeks are devoted to preparation of a paper which should deal with pedagogical or methodological issues of importance for the educational work of the trades unions and their members. These papers are often reports of a project, or field experiment, undertaken by one or more of the student teachers.

The target groups for this course are teachers, principals and librarians working in the labour movement, the folk high school movement and the study organisers and course leaders employed by the trade union movement itself.

Training study circle leaders in the Study Circle Associations

The eleven Study Circle Associations that are operational and receive governmental support are different in size, ideology and other aspects. The leadership (or *animateur*) training programmes vary considerably. Some of the associations have few full-time staff members and have difficulties in organising an adequate training programme for the pedagogical and administrative staff. Only a small minority of the study-circle leaders work full-time in this capacity whereas the vast majority undertake the role in their leisure time. It is necessary to be aware of this situation when describing and evaluating the training offered to circle leaders and other staff members of the Study Circle Associations.

Often the Study Circle Associations invite their study circle leaders to participate in two or three weekend courses in which they learn about the special aims of the organisation and about the educational philosophy of the particular study circle association, as well as receiving a general introduction to the other ten associations. Practical methods in teaching, as well as information on rules and administrative practice, are important on the courses offered to study circle leaders, as well as to other staff members.

The Study Circles Associations receive a special government grant to support their leadership training programmes and very often the course is organised in conjunction with a folk high school with which the association may share ideological or pedagogical concerns.

FURTHER EDUCATION AND IN-SERVICE TRAINING AND EDUCATION

In the programmes for staff development and study circle leader training in the Study Circle Associations there is no clear-cut division between pre-service and in-service training.

In the school system, including the folk high schools and municipal adult education, there is a special organisation for in-service training, which is attached to the regional university administration but which works in close contact with authorities in the field. Government grants are distributed among the six regional in-service training departments, but the greatest proportion of the money is transferred to the municipalities so that they can use it either to cover the learners' costs for participating in the courses arranged by those departments or to organise their own courses.

Currently, the majority of in-service training courses are staffed by university staff and the courses, to some extent, reflect the specialisms of the universities, with some being regional and others national, as is the case with the folk high school in-service courses organised by Linköping. As for municipal adult education, including adult basic education, all six regions are supposed to offer in-service training opportunities, but once again adult education has to compete with youth education for a share of the limited resources available for in-service training. In some respects, the Linköping In-Service Training department provides a nationwide service for municipal adult education, i.e. by publishing a newsletter *Kom*, informing teaching staff about opportunities for in-service training, further education and other means of professional development.

The folk high school training programme has some features which are worth noting:

1 Each academic year, at fixed periods, about thirty-five courses are offered to teaching staff, as well as to the students undertaking the full-time year of pre-service preparation, and this is also offered to other adult educators. Naturally these courses will run only if there is sufficient enrolment, so that probably only some twenty to twenty-five of these courses are actually offered in any one year. The costs of this programme are equally shared by the Teacher Training Programme and the In-Service Training department, while the participants' fees are normally covered by their employers or by the Teacher Training Programme where the teacher-students are concerned.

2 Each course is usually of one week's or two weeks' duration and is arranged in co-operation with different folk high schools or other institutions in different parts of Sweden or, since 1982, even beyond the national boundaries as some courses have been arranged in Denmark and Finland. There have also been courses in Norway, Holland, Austria and the United Kingdom and other courses with an international flavour are being organised, including one with Polish adult educators in co-operation with the Polish folk high school movement. Some of these courses are longer in duration, corresponding to five to ten weeks' study time, distributed over the whole year and sandwiching intense residential periods with some distance study and practice in the field.

3 Course themes tend to include: the interdependence between democracy and the non-formal adult education movement; the messages of pictures; computers — basic techniques and social effects; pedagogical drama and creativity (conducted in Finland); international meetings at such places as the People's International College in Denmark; song and dance in folk high school work; modern methods of language teaching; vocational guidance and counselling; teaching Swedish as a second language.

4 New themes may be proposed by anyone. Such proposals are evaluated and priorities are set by the staff and students from the folk high school course at Linköping, by a national steering committee, by the regional 'pedagogical secretaries' of the Swedish Union of Folk High School Teachers and Principals and by other interested bodies. The proposals are also discussed with the folk high school sector of the Swedish National Board of Education and eventually the decision is made by the governing board of the folk high school teacher training course, which was discussed earlier.

TRAINING OF TRAINERS AND RESEARCHERS

There is no pre-service training for the trainers other than that provided by the training/education of 'normal' adult educators or researchers. Considerable efforts, however, are dedicated to in-service training and to narrowing the gap between research and practice and researchers and practitioners.

An important aspect of the development in adult education as an independent area of research was the establishment of a Chair in Adult Education at Linköping in 1985, the only one in Sweden (with Professor Kjell Rubenson being the first holder), so that the development of a research staff and programme is still in its infancy. There are very many hopes but they will be impossible to meet without there being a considerable increase in the provision of resources. There has been a great deal of research in adult education in Sweden already, but it has not been possible previously to concentrate that work in a single institution in an exclusive adult education programme.

FUTURE DEVELOPMENTS

There are signs of a renewed debate on the role of adult education in Sweden. Parliament has laid down four goals for adult education:

* To promote democracy.
* To further an equal distribution of resources.
* To further the economic development of the country.
* To meet individual needs and interests.

The question of priorities between conflicting goals has been left open and this causes some uncertainty about the future development of adult education. If economic growth is to be the first priority, then technical and economic studies will become priority fields and educational opportunities will only be given to those people who are already well educated. If, on the other hand, the development of democracy and the equal distribution of resources (political, economic, cultural) are to be priorities, then there is a great deal of adult education research and development work, both formal and non-formal, essential to make it more capable of reaching the underprivileged groups. In this way they can be offered opportunities of learning and developing their own resources by unorthodox methods in order to stimulate self-reliance and creativity.

SUMMARY

Non-formal adult education has a long history in Sweden and at least one Swede in every three engages in some form of adult education every year. The largest number of courses and students are in the Study Circle Associations which are not bound by any pre-service training or education of the staff that they employ. In the folk high school movement, the normal pre-service education has become an academic degree but with teacher training not having been required until the 1970s. A special teacher training programme was established at Linköping in 1970 at what was then the Linköping Teacher Training College but which is now a university. Each year this offers the folk high school training as an independent course to seventy-five students, who must normally be graduates already or have at least five years' teaching experience.

Other training programmes for adult educators in the trade unions or other organisations of the labour movement are offered by the Trades Union Council. In addition, the Stockholm Teacher Training College offers training within its one-year courses for secondary school teachers.

On the whole, just a small proportion of all teachers working in adult education have had any pre-service or even in-service training in the teaching of adults. Recent developments may indicate a growing awareness of the need for specific measures to cope with this situation. The establishment of a professorship in adult education at Linköping is expected to prepare the ground for an increase in research and development in adult education which will be, hopefully, in close co-operation with practitioners in the field and with the already established teacher training programme.

The renewal of the ideological discussion about the priorities of the four goals of adult education, which are themselves supported by all political parties, will probably re-establish adult education as a central issue in political debate and action.

Part VI

Conclusions

17   Some current issues in the training of adult educators

Alan Chadwick

It is axiomatic that the term 'adult education' is commonly perceived to have various meanings. Is it as self-evident, despite the passage of time, that the following observation retains some currency?

> Almost any general assertion about the education of adults in the member countries of the Council of Europe, either collectively or individually, is open to challenge. Even more so when one speaks of training. The trouble is that the facts are incoherent to the point of chaos, and they are further complicated by partial initiatives towards rationalisation, and conflicting statements of ideological objective by voluntary organisations, governments and academic institutions.
>
> (Simpson 1976: 83)

As Simpson declares, there is neither an easily discernible entity known as 'adult education' nor of 'training'. Using a different term Duke, in discussing teacher education for adult educators includes for example '... industrial, commercial, and governmental training staff and other adult, continuing and non-formal education functionaries' (Duke 1989: 360).

Certainly, contributions to this volume have covered some of Duke's broad categories and have presented illustrations drawn from statutory, voluntary and private bases alike. Moreover, the general impression is that training opportunities have either been maintained or have grown as evidenced by the cases presented above. The term 'adult educator' is likewise capable of broad interpretation — *animateur*, teacher, instructor, coach, demonstrator, lecturer — while not disregarding managerial and support staff. The role, however it is defined, does not necessarily predispose individuals towards training or further training, as they may consider their existing subject knowledge as being sufficient proof of effectiveness.

As already indicated various forms of 'adult education' exist, ranging from programmes relating to liberal non-vocational study, and education which assists individuals to obtain different forms of qualification, to 'mixed media' provision and skills related to vocational training. But no one government agency deals with them all; this diffusion of responsibilities does not assist the development of an organised scheme of teacher training for adults. Simpson has suggested that:

> For the present . . . there can be little prospect of a rationalised, integrated system of training for adult education. Perhaps even in the long run it is too much to expect until there is a diminution of certain polarities in our societies . . . generally speaking, there is, on the one hand, a concept of adult education as a factor in social change, and, on the other, education in adapting to the existing order of things.
>
> (Simpson 1976: 87)

Nevertheless, training provision for adult educators, however incoherent or piecemeal, is increasingly being offered and a measure of co-operation adhered to as the preceding chapters indicate.

A major question concerns which groups, full- or part-time staff, should have priority in training. While not wishing to disregard the needs of full-time professionals, a particular focus has been placed on the position of part-time field-workers for they appear to form the majority of the workforce as described in the cases above.

An issue relating to the degree of importance ascribed to the work is that which concerns 'qualifications' and the forms and modes of training which certify individuals as being competent to teach adults. In order to ensure that training is of a high standard, irrespective of the form any qualification may take, the abilities of the trainer are of paramount importance. However, the diverse provision of training programmes for trainers appears to be increasing at varying rates in the public, private and voluntary sectors. In this regard universities, as one higher-education provider of training courses, may be perceived as having an increasingly important alongside part to play with other organisations which train adult educators to become effective practitioners.

Among issues which merit particular attention are those concerning the need for trained and qualified field-workers. Equally, the preparation and continuing development of trainers requires discussion. Most importantly, the question of legislation and the availability of resources to establish and support training provision must be addressed.

As both Irvine and Federighi indicate above, in chapters 4 and 8 respectively, the need for training adult educators has become an international affair, assisted to varying degrees by countries in and beyond Western Europe. Indications of concern have, for example, found some expression in the production of reports which have served to identify adult education training as an issue for discussion and, on occasion, a stimulant to action, as recorded by Legge in chapter 5. In broader terms legislation has taken account of professional and vocational education and training; this will be discussed later in the chapter.

A discernable momentum for change, which to an extent is vocationally driven, is also capable of other constructions and must take account of factors such as

. . . the tendency in much of West Europe to think of adult education as having an interventionist, quasi-political role demanding enthusiasm rather than skills. Many animateurs are committed to being agents of change . . . In Italy, the teachers of the '150 hours' movement have particular political and social views, and even non-political, non-denominational associations such as the Academy for Adult Education in Luzern, Switzerland, stress the value of education for social change. The result is some fear that organised forms of training would weaken 'commitment' and produce stereotyped, uninspiring, adult education workers.

(Legge 1985: 59-60)

In considering the present status of adult education the contribution of part-time adult educators, whether paid or voluntary, commands attention. In Belgium, where adult education is regarded as a part-time activity, part-timers form the largest group of workers, yet as Hinnekint notes in chapter 2, 'they are rarely offered training or re-training courses'. In Ireland most part-time adult educators seem to have received no training; in Norway most do not associate themselves with the field, seeing their work as being marginal; while in Greece part-timers do not appear to adapt their courses to students' needs due to lack of training.

In common with a number of other countries, part-time adult educators are in the majority in Finland. However, only a minority have received training. As Bax notes:

The involvement of part-timers, who very often teach in

their own time in adult education and have full-time functions in other sectors of society, makes it possible for adult education to keep close to new developments and interests. Very often, however, part-timers do not have enough background in educational work and there is a strong need for training in this field.

(Bax 1989: 403)

Some initiatives have been taken; a form of training takes place in Austria, while in the Federal Republic of Germany courses have been developed, with university involvement, to qualify part-time adult educators. Similarly, Swiss provision includes '... a Diploma in Adult Education ... aimed at part-time tutors' which is offered at the Academy for Adult Education in Lucerne.

In the above discussions issues surrounding status, and professionalisation, find a natural focus in training which is formally accredited. As well as 'qualifications' gained through on-the-job experience or attendance at non-award-bearing courses, the issue of credentials has been referred to by a number of contributors to this volume, albeit with reference to full-time as well as part-time adult educators, employed as teachers or trainers, in both vocational and general adult education. For example, adult educators may be subject qualified, but have no formal educational qualifications beyond having taken a study unit in andragogy or pedagogy, together with practice teaching, as in vocational education training in Finland. In France *animateurs* can obtain diplomas yet no national award exists for youth or adult trainers. Involvement in non-formal education of adults in the Netherlands does not require workers to acquire formal qualifications; this is also the position in the United Kingdom, while in the Danish centres for teachers in adult education teaching qualifications 'are beginning to emerge' although it remains true that adult education is still the one area of teaching 'where there is no statutory requirement to have undertaken a course before employment'.

Where qualifications are required for teaching adults this may simply depend on the possession of a degree, or a school teaching qualification, as in Belgium where '... little or no thought is given to training for work in the field of adult education'. However, in Norway, given that university entrance requirements are met, students can study part-time for a Certificate in Adult Education. Exceptionally, the possession of a relevant qualification may even prove to be an impediment. In the Federal Republic of Germany a Diploma in Pedagogics can be taken with adult education as a specialist option. However, holders of this particular award face the probability of rejection by adult education institutes which prefer individuals with 'teachable' subjects.

Where training programmes are being planned questions arise as to the most effective type of provision, i.e. pre-service, in-service or advanced. In some cases there may be no clear division between one type or another as in certain forms of training in Sweden. Many factors have to be taken into account, not least scarcity of resources. Recidivism can occur, as in other types of educational provision, whereby a lack of continuing post-training support and staff development may produce a falling away of an individual's competence and motivation. Other questions include a concern for mode(s) of training. In the United Kingdom the Open University has developed distance and independent training opportunities, referred to by Legge. Similarly, in the Federal Republic of Germany self-study courses have been developed by the Folk High Schools Association in conjunction with adult educators and university staff.

The role played by the higher education sector in the training of adult educators, particularly the universities, has been referred to consistently throughout the volume. While focusing some attention on universities the contribution of other major institutions: polytechnics, academies, colleges of higher education and teacher training bodies, must also be recognised. For example, those academies with responsibility for training school teachers in Austria have gained Ministry of Education approval to establish additional courses for students wishing to teach adults.

The involvement of universities in training adult educators inevitably differs from country to country. In some a close link with the field has been established, as in the cases of the Federal Republic of Germany and the United Kingdom. In Italy provision is mainly concerned with the basic training of practitioners. As Federighi notes, such training exists '... in the universities of Arezzo, Cosenza, Florence, Rome, Padova and Palermo, where the students have the opportunity to study the theory, history and methodology of adult education.'

In others, such as Norway, adult education is yet to be fully integrated with universities and, therefore, discussion must concentrate both upon adult education as a discipline or field, and the role of universities and colleges of higher education with regard to the training of adult educators. In Greece a role is sought whereby '... the systematic training of adult educators, both in teaching methods and professional socialisation, requires

211

the universities to co-operate with the institutions of continuing education'.

In the same way an expectation, identified in the contribution from Belgium, is that universities should give some thought to an adult education component within secondary school teacher training programmes; despite the expansion of adult education in Belgium this has not yet been forthcoming.

Other forms of recent or current co-operation include that of Barcelona University where, in recent collaboration with an external organisation, a training course was offered in order to prepare unemployed Spanish graduates as adult educators. With regard to the training of trainers, yet here, as with other themes, there is little consistency. In France, for example, the majority of adult educators practise '... as though it were tacitly assumed that people entering upon the work of continuing training did not need to have received it themselves'. University adult educators, among others in higher education, are not exempt from this criticism, particularly when the status accorded to them by field-workers is taken into account. It is ironic that university adult educators, as trainers and trainers of trainers, appear, in the main, not to have been trained themselves, either formally or via in-service training. It has already been noted, for example, that the possession of a degree is seen in some quarters as sufficient proof of adult educational competence. It appears to be the exception rather than the rule that university staff employed as adult educators are themselves appropriately qualified. A comparison may be drawn with staff in teacher training institutions who are generally assumed to have been trained as educators as a basis for preparing others.

With reference to training Pfluger observes that:

> . . . adult educators, not excluding those working in universities, should themselves have deep and constantly renewed experience of work for which they train others. Teachers in higher education and others engaged in training adult educators should be given the opportunity of themselves practising regularly in the field: indeed, this should be made an obligation.
>
> (Pfluger 1978: 48)

It should be indisputable that in order to ensure a high standard of provision for students, trainees, employees and others engaged in varying forms of adult education, training for adult educators is a necessity. It is also posited that training trainers' programmes are an essential first stage in establishing and maintaining excellence of provision.

There appears to be general agreement that more attention should be paid to training trainers and that such provision should be continuing, irrespective of whether it is concerned with general or vocational adult education. At some point rhetoric should find an outcome in action yet there are general anxieties surrounding the central issue of resource provision, despite the growth of adult education discerned by some contributors.

As proposed earlier, legislation is a critical factor in the quest for resources. In describing the main elements of the wide-ranging but not totally inclusive Norwegian Adult Education Act, 1976, Brattset comments that 'the mere existence of the Act is important. Legislation represents a recognition of the field and puts adult education on an equal footing with other parts of the educational system'. In Norway a major financial contribution is provided by the state towards the supplying of adult education services, but 'Despite variations in legal, financial and organisational measures, it is felt that there is a need to consider the whole field as a unity, to meet demands and solve problems which are common to all sections.' Arguably, this concept of a systematised and coherent structure is praiseworthy, implying as it does equality of opportunity for a wide range of individuals and groups. Whether it can become a reality is a matter for debate.

In the recent past some opportunities for the production of legislation supportive to adult education have been missed: in 1986 the Swedish government, in passing an act concerning qualifications for teachers of Swedish to young people and adult immigrants, made no mention of the need for any related adult education training. Two reports were produced in Ireland, in 1973 and 1984, which raised expectations among adult educators but did not, in fact, produce any substantial change. A proposal for establishing a law for adult education was put forward by the Italian Association for Adult Education in 1987 without success. Federighi argues on p. 113 that such a law is required as it '... would lay the institutional foundations necessary to cope with problems of status, role and professionalism of the practitioners'.

In Cyprus law 21/74 established the Industrial Training Authority. While this was significant in the development of vocational adult education Symeonides argues above that

> Cyprus has not yet taken any legislative measures nor promoted any structures to support non-vocational adult education, so that the development of a comprehensive system of adult education to promote the general well-being

of the people and to further individual growth and development has not yet been established.

There is evidence, however, of some support for aspects of adult education. In Belgium socio-cultural adult education is government funded, as is the training of study circle leaders in Sweden. To this degree, although overall provision remains discordant, there is some indication of progress, either with initiatives being supported by governments or, as in the case of recently developed training schemes for British part-time teachers of adults, through action being taken despite lack of interest at governmental level.

In Spain the General Education Act 1970 established *educacion permanente* as a reality, while in France a major Law of 1971 on Continuing Education closely affected adult education and resulted in more direct intervention by the state than had previously been the case. As Bolhuis and Wagenaar report in chapter 3, a General Act on Adult Education in the Netherlands has passed through parliament; and, among other measures, a 'coherent support system' is to be established for adult education provision. Similarly, higher vocational education, which deals with various forms of vocational training relevant to adult education, has been regulated by a new law since 1986. In Denmark an education act of 1968 ensures the provision of education for young people and adults although, in identifying some of its weaknesses, Haüser points towards inequalities such as the need for a clearer view on and commitment to equal opportunities and outreach provision; an experimental programme is currently under way with a brief to identify a need for legislative 'revision' of this act.

In reviewing adult education legislation in Western Europe Stock identifies differences due, in part, to the dissimilarities between nations, but notes that

> The importance of professional and vocational education and training is underlined by the volume of legislation specifically devoted to it. Austria, Denmark, Finland, the Federal Republic of Germany, France, Italy, the Netherlands, Portugal, Spain, Sweden, Switzerland and the United Kingdom all have such laws.
>
> (Stock 1989: 482)

More specifically,

Austria, Denmark, England and Wales, Hesse, Lower Saxony,

Saarland and France all have sections of law or regulations allowing for the promotion, support and requirement for either initial or in-service training or [*sic*] full time or part-time staff.

(Stock 1989: 484)

This situation should not be underrated given the general observation that current economic problems

. . . have tempered the full execution of the legislation as enacted in the various countries [of Western Europe]. Instead of working towards a comprehensive provision of adult education, governments now tend to choose programmes dealing with the effects of the economic crisis, and priority is given to specific projects.

(Bax 1989: 402)

The inauguration of the Single European Market, with its socio-economic thrust, will, however, have a direct bearing on this issue and is discussed below. Despite uneven patterns of legislation, there are some commonly recognised training goals and requests for co-operation between countries.

Reviews of adult education and its teacher education, both scholarly studies and international conferences, largely agree in calling for much more massive and systematic training, including co-operation and rationalization between kinds of institutions and programmes.

(Duke 1989: 368)

In practice, the position identified by Freynet may not be very far removed from that of neighbouring countries in Western Europe. In France, diversity of provision ranges

. . . from the activist of popular education to the training specialist of the firm, where the emphasis swings between education and human resource management . . . [and] the lack of a clearly defined status for the trainer and the highly differentiated functions of the adult educators.

At the same time, examples can be found where common ground has been recognised; long-standing links have existed between Belgium and Holland as noted by Hinnekint.

As Kasimir indicates, the Swedish Folk High School in-service training programme includes courses held in Austria,

Denmark, Finland, Holland, Norway and the United Kingdom. These examples of inter-country co-operation do not deny the point made by Knitter-Lux with reference to Austria, that within countries there is a need for adult education bodies to work more closely together. In this regard the role of the European Bureau of Adult Education is centrally important in stimulating exchanges of views and practices, and assisting and informing adult education organisations through meetings, conferences and publications.

> In the years of its existence the Bureau's work has been based on the fact that its associates in various countries found themselves confronted with similar educational problems, and were willing to find co-operative solutions. This has been true not only in periods of economic growth, but also — and is perhaps even more the case — in periods of economic difficulty when the need to find creative answers to common problems has increased.
>
> (Bax 1989: 462)

With the Single European Market in mind an impending issue may concern a wider recognition of adult education qualifications and, concomitantly raise, questions such as optional or obligatory training for all adult educators and the 'crediting' of awards in education such as those held by school teachers wishing to train as adult educators. Equally, any moves towards 'professionalisation' would require debate. For example, would such initiatives appear to be '... a necessary component in the organisation of a systematic programme for the training of adult educators' as suggested by Vergidis? Would periodic re-training be entailed as suggested by Hinnekint and Weinberg?

A related topic is that of research; Weinberg argues for '... research based on knowledge and skills to enable adult educators to stimulate two-way learning processes. We need more learning teachers and teaching learners than we have at the moment'. It is further argued that more systematic research in key areas such as women's education and inter-cultural learning will also be required.

The establishment of the Single European Market will have an increasing impact on, and create opportunities for, education and training provision for adults. Accordingly, the European Bureau of Adult Education will doubtless expect to play its part in this sphere. There are many issues to be considered, including that of mobility; individuals holding certain professional qualifications will have freedom of movement within the

European Community and this will result in greater concordance regarding their acceptance. However, in this context it should be noted that establishing the comparability of qualifications does not imply their mutual recognition.

Other factors relate to modes of delivery such as modularised programmes, self-access learning units, satellite and computer links, and an expanded use of open and distance learning materials. Arguably, a major task for the European Bureau will be the creation of opportunities for discussion between its member nations and other interested parties of the Single European Market's effect on vocational and general training of adult educators. One directly relevant topic might concern the development of transnational training programmes which could attract joint accreditation.

At a time of specific change and particular opportunity McNair, writing in a British context, offers a timely if cautionary set of observations which update Simpson's comments noted above.

> Over the next decade demographic, social, economic and technological change will lead to a rapid expansion in demand for education and training for adults and in demand for the skills of those with experience of facilitating adult learning. However, this does not imply a simple expansion of what currently exists. While, by one means or another, the growing demand will be met, it is difficult to predict the shape of the new system, in terms of the mix of public, private and voluntary sector providers, of modes of delivery and institutional structures. Similarly, while there are strong pressures for the expansion of education and training for adults, this will not automatically lead to access for all, although any would wish to see this, for pragmatic or idealistic reasons. Neither skill shortages, technological change nor demography will in themselves lead to a more equitable distribution of educational opportunity.
>
> (McNair 1989: 5)

The case studies presented above represent their authors' personal and professional views regarding the state of training in their respective countries. Inevitably, problems, opportunities and successes emerge showing characteristics of their own national situations. While recognising the dangers of generalising from the particular, a number of common aspirations and trends can be recognised. In broad terms they point towards the need for a more comprehensive and harmonious approach to training, based

217

on various forms of self-interest, and relate, inevitably, to prevailing tendencies such as socio-economic, demographic and technological changes. These aspirations and trends also point to a requirement for functional co-operation between paymasters, providers and recipients of training in all spheres and wherever collaboration is mutually desirable and achievable. In some countries efforts have been made to institute closer working relationships between different sectors so that in France, for example, continuing training is co-ordinated by the Ministry of Vocational Training.

Some unification of provision between those agencies which provide and those which pay for training could represent an important first step towards a more coherent form of provision in countries where high quality training of adults is, or is due to become, an expanding service industry, and where the preparation, development and support of those with training responsibilities is pivotal. Grabowski's comment, albeit from an American perspective, may be pertinent.

> Until recent years, each organisation or agency found its own way in training. Now the fundamental similarities among various types of training are recognised, and many trainers see a value in working closely with others to advance the state of the art of training.
>
> (Grabowski 1981: 134)

BIBLIOGRAPHY

Bax, W. (1989) 'Provision in Western Europe', in Titmus, Colin J. (ed.) *Lifelong Education for Adults*, Oxford: Pergamon.

Duke, C. (1989) 'Training of adult educators' in Titmus, Colin J. (ed.) *Lifelong Education for Adults*, Oxford: Pergamon.

Grabowski, Stanley M. *et al.* (1981) *Preparing Educators of Adults*, San Francisco: Jossey Bass.

Legge, Derek (1985) 'Training of adult education workers', in *Convergence*, vol. XVIII, nos. 3-4.

McNair, Stephen (1989) 'Trends and issues in education and training for adults', *Discussion Paper*, Unit for the Development of Adult Continuing Education.

Pfluger, A. (1978) *Training and Re-training of Adult Educators*, Strasbourg: Council for Cultural Co-operation of the Council of Europe.

Simpson, James A. (1976/7) 'Some general trends in the training of teachers of adults in Western Europe', in *Society and Leisure*, vol. 18, part 4.

Stock, A. (1989) 'Adult education legislation in Western Europe', in Titmus, Colin J. (ed.) *Lifelong Education for Adults*, Oxford: Pergamon.

Appendices

1 Training adult educators in Cyprus

Klitos Symeonides

It is difficult for a Cypriot researcher to present such a study as this because in Cyprus adult education, and particularly the training of adult educators, is faced with many limitations. Both the lack of literature related to this, as well as a clear structure to adult education makes it a difficult undertaking. There is, in addition, a lack of tradition in adult education as well as the absence of trained adult educators. This latter factor inhibits training initiatives.

ADULT EDUCATION IN CYPRUS

For the whole of its long history Cyprus has been under foreign domination. Both its wealth and its strategic position have made it an object of contest among the great powers in the area. It was only in 1960 that Cyprus gained its independence from the United Kingdom and the island was proclaimed a republic. Before independence, adult education was almost totally lacking and the country was agrarian, with the few technical skills being obtained through the traditional system of apprenticeship. After independence, adult education was given much greater emphasis, for a variety of reasons:

1 There was a new emphasis upon economic advancement. Five-year plans were drawn up and the importance of work-orientated skills, not only among the young, was stressed. Hence, vocational training was given high priority.
2 Cultural and community development programmes assumed great significance, especially after the 1974 invasion by the Turks when 40 per cent of the population became refugees. Maintenance of morale, the need for social cohesion among the refugees and the prevention of cultural underdevelopment were all reasons for the expansion.
3 New administrative and other jobs were established in the

221

expanding social and economic structure of Cyprus, as it moved towards industrialisation.

By the end of 1973, Cyprus had begun to provide a sound infrastructure for an adult education provision. It had established such institutions as a pedagogical institute for in-service training programmes mainly for teachers of primary and secondary education, evening gymnasia for second-chance education, evening technical classes for training and re-training, etc. In addition, the establishment in 1973 of an Inter-Ministerial Youth Committee, co-ordinating the Ministries of Agriculture and of Labour, was a significant step forward. However, thirteen years of planned development (1960-1973) was brought to an abrupt halt in July 1974 when Cyprus was invaded, divided and 40 per cent of the people displaced.

THE PRESENT SITUATION

The unstable political situation after the invasion and the consequent cultural, social and economic constraints delayed the development of a sound system of adult education. While Cyprus had produced a formal school system which can be compared to the educational standards of advanced countries, adult education has not been developed. Yet a great deal of adult education occurs in Cyprus although the programmes face many problems related to the limitations of organisation and administration.

Programmes provided for adults have the following characteristics:

1   There are a great number of providers in both the statutory and voluntary sectors. In the area of vocational adult education, for instance, the main providers are:

- The Industrial Training Authority, which identifies the specific needs in manpower, develops training systems and policies and promotes measures for their effective implementation by means of systematic training.
- The Productivity Centre, which assists private and public enterprises to increase their productivity by means of management development, supervisory and vocational training.
- The Higher Technical Institute, which offers three-year courses in electrical engineering, civil engineering, mechanical engineering and computer studies.

- The Hotel and Catering Institute, which offers a three-year course in cookery and one-year courses in reception, waiting and housekeeping.

In terms of second-chance education there are three evening gymnasia in the three main cities which provide a secondary education leaving certificate. The foreign-language institutes and evening technical classes offer courses in foreign languages, commercial subjects and technical training. In the adult education centres there is a main programme in general, non-certificated adult education. The youth centres and the agricultural extension classes offer leisure-time and mainly recreational activities. Parent education, social, political and religious education, as well as the education of workers, are all provided by a variety of voluntary bodies.

2 All the above programmes run independently of one another. There is no co-ordinating mechanism for bringing together the various providers and this sometimes results in fragmentation and incoherence of provision.
3 Most of the institutions are in the cities and the rural population have no adequate access to learning opportunities.
4 The people attending the programmes are usually the most stimulated and active members of their age groups and they tend to have had a sound initial education. By contrast, those in most need are not so highly motivated and tend not to participate.
5 The narrow range and diversity of activities do not meet the needs and interests of specific groups in the population, so that large groups, e.g. the armed forces, the elderly, the disadvantaged and those living in the rural areas could all be offered more educational help.

The enactment of law 21/74, in which the Industrial Training Authority was established, was an important step in the development of vocational adult education. However, Cyprus has not yet taken any legislative measures nor promoted any structure to support non-vocational adult education, so that the development of a comprehensive system of adult education to promote the general well-being of the people and to further individual growth and development has not yet been established.

THE TRAINING OF ADULT EDUCATORS

There is no cadre of tutors or administrators serving adult education in Cyprus although the lack of training provision in adult education has been identified. Melo (1982) made the following comment: 'The training of adult educators is virtually non-existent in Cyprus' and Robin Usher (1984, reported in 1985) observed, 'In my opinion, the greatest area of need in adult education in Cyprus is for the training of adult educators at different levels.'

It is of interest to the present study to examine the training activities offered to adult educators serving in the main non-formal education programmes in Cyprus, e.g. the adult education centres of the Ministry of Education and the training offered by the Industrial Training Authority.

Adult education centres

These centres serve about 8,000 adults every year but there is no cadre of tutors or administrators. The headmaster of the school where the centre is located is automatically the principal of the centre, although no extra payment is received for this. Principals make enrolments, plan the programme, train tutors, collect fees and undertake every other activity in relation to the centre.

Before 1974 all tutors were primary school teachers but, currently, more than 80 per cent of them are subject-orientated tutors. There is no scheme of service for appointment, nor for systematic supervision and evaluation of tutors. The centre personnel (principal and tutors) do not receive any training to work with adults, although a few two to three hour seminars are organised occasionally. These tend to concentrate upon matters of organisation.

The Pedagogical Academy of Cyprus (the teacher training college has, in the past few years) organised a course for those third-year students who wish to work with adults. This is a part-time course of four three-quarters of an hour periods a week through the year and is considered a significant step in training some teachers who will work with adults.

In 1985 and 1986, the Ministry of Education, in co-operation with the Pedagogical Institute, organised long training courses (twenty periods of forty-five minutes) for tutors working at the adult education centres, mainly to train them in adult psychology, group dynamics and organisational matters.

Industrial Training Authority

This was established by the law 21/74. It is the major instrument for training and re-training the employed and the unemployed in the country. The introduction of a system of financing its training programmes, based upon a contribution, e.g. 0.5 per cent of the total wage-bill, contributes to the further development of the Authority. The main provisions made by legislation include the organisation and supervision of training schools and training courses, the setting of standards of industrial training and providing payment of training allowances to employers.

The Industrial Training Authority is a semi-governmental organisation responsible for the training, and the channelling into the economy, of personnel at all levels on the basis of identified needs, so that the authority confines its activities to training and not to education. All the programmes of the authority may be classified as adult education programmes, but their basic characteristic is their direct relation to the needs of the economy and the supply of specialised knowledge and skills required by people who are being recruited into specific trades and occupations.

It must, of course, be recognised that the authority itself is not a training establishment but a central organisation whose aim is to co-ordinate and implement an island-wide system of training. In the pursuit of this role the authority co-operates with both the state and private-sector training establishments and also with other enterprises which train their own personnel. The authority is of the opinion that if organisations are convinced of the benefits of training personnel, and they undertake it for themselves, then this will be of benefit to the community as a whole. To achieve this end the authority is already undertaking a programme of 'training the trainers' courses in industry, which offers to employees the knowledge and skill necessary to provide training at the following levels:

1 training job instructors,
2 training trainers,
3 training training officers.

Some 270 personnel in the hotel and catering and in the clothing industries had been through this programme by the end of 1985 and in 1986 a further twenty-eight programmes (clothing, furniture, metal, footwear and, especially, the rapidly expanding hotel industry) were held.

TRAINING — THE FUTURE

The training of adult educators is a key matter in the development of adult education in Cyprus and this, it could be argued, depends upon the creation of a nucleus of key adult educators. As society in general and policy-makers in particular are not aware of the potential contribution of adult educators to the social, economic, political and cultural development of this country, the importance of training is even more crucial. The diversity of training needs is obvious. Those with multiple roles (organisers, administrators, etc.), managers of adult education provision (curriculum developers, researchers, etc.) student members and ancillary staff (clerical, catering, portering) need different kinds of training. Policy-makers and planners need training in order to become aware of the objectives and potential of adult education.

Some important decisions need to be taken in the future concerning training initiatives. The following are some suggestions:

1   The Pedagogical Academy of Cyprus (teacher training college) and the Pedagogical Institute should be the main institutions for training adult educators.
2   The curriculum of the Pedagogical Academy should be extended to include adult education. All the students should have, during their initial training, the opportunity to acquire skills and knowledge in working with adults. Future school teachers should be ready to work as adult educators, community educators or community leaders.
3   Teachers of secondary education should, during their preparatory year at the Pedagogical Institute, be given training in adult education, teaching and programme planning.
4   The training of trainers is a very important issue and collective efforts should be made by both the academy and the institute to crate a special group of adult trainers. A full-time cadre of educators is necessary in order to take up key positions as organisers, administrators, curriculum developers, etc. To this effect more effort should be made by the government for the preparation of specialists to undertake the above roles, using the assistance of foreign experts if necessary.
5   The possibility of training adult educators abroad should be seriously considered. With the present lack of expertise among local training staff any programme for training adult

trainers and full-time adult educators should be run jointly by the academy and the institute, with the assistance of adult educators from abroad.

6 The training of subject-orientated tutors could be undertaken at regional and local levels giving emphasis to in-service and on-the-job training.

7 The development of methods of teaching and learning, as well as how to organise classes, plan programmes, skills in publicising courses, etc. might all be included in a programme of training the trainers and training full-time adult educators.

The present overall picture may not be satisfactory, but there is an awareness about the problems and efforts are being made to improve the situation.

BIBLIOGRAPHY

Melo, A. (1982) *Structures and Strategies for Adult Education*, Cyprus: UNESCO.

Usher, R. (1985) Report on a Visit to Cyprus (unpublished). See *Industrial Training Authority Annual Report*.

2 The European Bureau of Adult Education

Bill Bax

The European Bureau of Adult Education was established by the European Cultural Centre in Geneva in 1958: it is a non-governmental organisation which acts as a forum for organisations in the field of adult and continuing education. Associates of the Bureau comprise the national co-ordinating bodies for adult education in various countries in Europe, and it provides research and documentation and is concerned about the training of adult educators. Its total membership is 160 different organisations in eighteen countries.

The registered office of the Bureau is in the Netherlands, and its address is: Nieuweweg 4, PO Box 367, 3800 AJ Amersfoort, The Netherlands. Its expenses are covered by membership fees, subsidies from national governments and grants from governments and international organisations.

As a forum for exchange and co-operation the bureau organises numerous meetings and conferences about many subjects including residential adult education, rural development, policies for training adult educators and the relationship between adult education and industrial training. More recently, such subjects as educational leave and specific target groups such as illiterates, the unemployed and women have all been focused on in the work of the Bureau.

During the period 1987 to 1990 the attention of many of the member organisations of the Bureau has been directed towards the effects of the economic situation in their respective countries and the results of the introduction of new information technology. A number of reports on these subjects have already been published by the Bureau, and this has led to a large project throughout the whole of Europe being undertaken. This has the general title of *Education and Training of Adults in a Changing Employment Market*. The whole project has been supervised by an international steering committee, and has four parts: education and training of adults and changing patterns of employment in southern and northern Europe; answering the needs for education and training of specific groups of unemployed adults who encounter special difficulties; educational institutions and agencies and the employment market and specific working methods. It is hoped that there will be a final report on the whole project by the end of 1990, but there have already been a number of interim reports concerning various aspects of this work.

Index

Index